Capital Kings

The 25 Greatest High School Players from Washington, D.C., and their Stories

Josh Barr
with
Bob Geoghan

authorHOUSE®

AuthorHouse™
1663 Liberty Drive
Bloomington, IN 47403
www.authorhouse.com
Phone: 1 (800) 839-8640

Published by AuthorHouse   10/16/2015

ISBN: 978-1-4772-7332-6 (sc)
ISBN: 978-1-4772-7331-9 (hc)
ISBN: 978-1-4772-7330-2 (e)

Library of Congress Control Number: 2012917634

Print information available on the last page.

Any people depicted in stock imagery provided by Thinkstock are models,
and such images are being used for illustrative purposes only.
Certain stock imagery © *Thinkstock.*

This book is printed on acid-free paper.

Contents

Foreword

Washington, D.C., is known for many things, and one of those is the incredible place that high school basketball holds in this area. I'm not saying it is bigger than the President, the White House or the Washington Monument. But as much as the city is known for its monuments and great institutions, Washington also is known for its high school basketball.

When I look back to a guy like Red Auerbach saying, "High school basketball in Washington -- there is none better," that gets your attention.

You think back: The first NCAA championship was held in the late 1930s, there I was playing high school basketball in the late 1940s and it was really just starting to gain ground. Then you see those first great players to burst onto the scene: Jack George and Elgin Baylor. They were two of the founding fathers of Washington, D.C., basketball, really you might say.

I'll bet you that we've had as many, if not more, NBA players come out of our high schools than from any other similar geographic area in terms of size. I'm not saying Washington against the state of California. But eighteen of them have come out of DeMatha alone. Baylor and Dave Bing, both from Spingarn; it goes on and on. You know how narrow that pyramid gets at the top? Think about how many college players have come from this area. Out of DeMatha alone, it is more than 200. This has become a remarkably fertile recruiting ground.

You think of some of the legendary games that have been played here. The 1966 NCAA championship game featuring Texas Western against Kentucky at Cole Field House. Stop and think: It has nothing to do with high school basketball, but a lot of historic things have happened here. Red made it his home. John Thompson was the first African American to coach a national college champ. There are a lot of firsts.

This obviously is such a special place for high school basketball, and these twenty-five players help to tell it.

Not a day goes by that I'm not asked about former players and games. It's amazing the number of people who come up and say they were at Cole Field House on January 30, 1965, when we beat Lew Alcindor (now known as Kareem Abdul-Jabbar) and Power Memorial, ending its 71-game winning streak. They'll talk about other games, other events – "I was there the night this happened or that happened," And so on. Or they will ask if I was there the night something in particular happened.

My wife, Kathy, and I talk about how in this area, when you meet someone and talk and realize they are from here, you always ask, "Where did you go to high school?" You don't ask where they went to college. And automatically, it switches to basketball.

I visited this guy in a nursing home and he introduced me to his roommate, and I immediately asked where he went to high school. And I was embarrassed because he didn't go to high school. But you always ask that question and then want to talk basketball out of that question.

Without a doubt, the two games with Power Memorial were the greatest high school games played. You had Alcindor, both games selling out Cole Field House. Two high school teams doing that? That is hard to do. It really elevated high school basketball to another level. *Time* magazine and other media outlets were there. From that time on, people took notice of high school basketball all over the country. It blossomed into a national discussion. Where did that start? In Washington.

There is nothing like competition to bring out the best and to have everybody striving to be the best.

I can think back to when I was in high school and even coached two years at St. Joe's and three years at St. John's. Nobody was playing basketball in the summer. Kids did not play basketball in the summer. Then Joe Gallagher and I started the Metropolitan Area Basketball School. It was the first daytime basketball camp in the country and the second basketball camp in the country -- there was an overnight one in the Poconos. Joe asked me if kids would play during the day and I said we would see. Most folks figured that in the summer, people weren't going to play basketball. That's another thing that mushroomed -- kids playing basketball in the summer.

There are so many great players from Washington, it is mind-boggling. You have problems picking the best twenty-five. But if you wanted to pick the best five players, it would be a real dogfight. We have three of them in the Hall of Fame. And we'll have five in a few years. How many high schools have two? Spingarn did -- Baylor and Bing. Then you have the coach-player combination in myself and Adrian Dantley. Thompson is in as a coach, but he also played and coached at St. Anthony High School. Dallas Shirley was a referee. And Red, of course.

One thing that really more than anything helped this area was Red. I'm a sophomore at Montgomery Blair High School in Silver Spring, Maryland, in 1947-48, and I'm on the jayvee team, and who comes out to scrimmage the varsity? Red brings the Washington Capitols, the professional team he was coaching, from the old Uline Arena. I'm watching from the stands. Ray Luckett makes a basket and Red runs out with a contract, pen and paper, like he's going to sign him on the spot. It was a big show.

Red, more than anybody else, got the whole idea jump-started. I'm sure we were not the only high school he visited.

He came here and planted a seed -- planted a bunch of seeds, really.

Picture this: We have the first day basketball camp in the country, and who speaks to the campers once a week because he has a regular tennis game in the adjacent tennis courts? Red.

Red got Bob Cousy to come to camp, and Cousy says, "Who is that guy guarding me? He's not bad." And I tell him, "Well, that's Dave Bing. He's going to be pretty good."

Basketball in Washington became a year-round thing, no question. Imagine having James Brown or Dantley knocking on your door on Christmas Day to get a key to the gym. It's 365 days a year, no doubt.

I remember coaching in the Jelleff Summer League all-star game one year. The game matched our DeMatha team against the Interhigh All-Stars – the top players from the D.C. public school league. People were hanging on the roofs, phone poles -- anywhere they could get to see the game. We lost in three overtimes by one point. Afterward, I was fishing for a compliment from Red, who had sat on our bench the whole night and heard me during every timeout. But he didn't say a thing.

The next day, I was at camp at St. John's and he came by to play tennis. So I asked again what he thought of the game and he said, "You lost the feel of the game. If you're going to be a coach, you can't be a spectator. You have to know what is really going on out there." It fits everything in life. It doesn't matter where you are in life: Do you know where you are in the game?

Some of the things that were great have been passed by, such as the old Washington Star tournament at Ritchie Coliseum. You can never get it again because of the various state rules, but it was the two best teams from Maryland, two from Virginia, two from the Interhigh, two from the

Catholic league. I guarantee there couldn't be another place in the country drawing a tournament like that. Geographically, you couldn't pull that off. Washington, our nation's capital, could be the nation's basketball capital. That was the forerunner to the Knights of Columbus Tournament.

I'm not saying here is where it happened first. But go back to the 1950s, when the good athletes played several sports. Gradually, though, if a guy's game was basketball, that was all he played. Dantley was a perfect example. He played football as a junior; he was a tight end and he was incredible. That summer, he was talking to Red and said he was playing both sports. And Red says, "Eh, going to play professionally in both sports? Let me show you how much you can make in each sport." So Adrian stuck with basketball.

In Washington, politics is a way of life, but basketball is a way of life, too.

Morgan Wootten
Coach, DeMatha Catholic High School, 1956 to 2002
Inducted into the Naismith Memorial Basketball Hall of Fame,
October 2000

Introduction

How do you pick and then rank the twenty-five best basketball players from the Washington area?

It was not easy.

There was no formula.

For starters, a player had to play his high school basketball locally. His high school career, college career and professional career all were taken into consideration, but there was no set equation for determining the list.

Former coaches, current coaches and many of the players themselves were asked their opinions.

Ask any number of people, though, and you are likely to get that same number of different answers. For in the Washington area, picking the Capital Kings is the longtime barbershop debate. For every case made, there is a rebuttal that is just as strong and equally passionate.

Some players went on to greatness in the college or professional levels but never starred in high school.

Steve Francis (Montgomery Blair, 1996) never played varsity basketball in high school, though he was the second overall pick in the 1999 NBA draft, the 2000 rookie of the year and a three-time NBA all-star.

Similarly, David Robinson (Osbourn Park, 1983) was a ten-time NBA all-star and a member of the league's Fiftieth Anniversary all-time team. But he did not play organized basketball until his senior year of high school, when he made all-district but was not close to being All-Met.

Others on the "honorable mention" list, who can be found on plenty of other Best-Of lists, include:

Hymie Perlo, Theodore Roosevelt, 1941; Tom Hoover, Archbishop Carroll, 1959.

John Thompson, Carroll, 1960; Fred Hetzel, Landon, 1961; Marty Lentz, Mount Vernon, 1961; John Austin, DeMatha, 1962; Bobby Lewis, St. John's, 1963; Skeeter Swift, George Washington, 1965; John Hummer, Washington-Lee, 1966; Tom Little, Mackin, 1966; Sid Catlett, DeMatha, 1967; Gary Browne, Whitman, 1968; Harold Fox, Northwestern, 1968; Jim O'Brien, Stuart, 1969.

Ed Peterson, Springbrook, 1970; Buzzy Braman, Springbrook, 1973; Eddie Jordan, Carroll, 1973; Lovell "Slim" Joiner, Eastern, 1974; Donald "Duck" Williams, Mackin 1974; Brian Magid, Blair, 1975; Billy Bryant, Carroll, 1976; John "Bay-Bay" Duren, Dunbar, 1976; Craig Shelton, Dunbar, 1976; Charles "Hawkeye" Whitney, DeMatha, 1976; Tracy Jackson, Paint Branch, 1977; Thurl Bailey, Bladensburg 1979; Sidney Lowe, DeMatha, 1979; Dereck Whittenburg, DeMatha, 1979.

Tom Sluby, Gonzaga, 1980; Adrian Branch, DeMatha, 1981; Anthony Jones, Dunbar, 1981; Carlos Yates, Flint Hill, 1981; Michael Jackson, South Lakes, 1982; Tommy Amaker, W.T. Woodson, 1983; Darryl Prue, Dunbar, 1985; Mark Tillmon, Gonzaga, 1986; Hubert Davis, Lake Braddock, 1988; Arron Bain, Flint Hill, 1989; George Lynch, Flint Hill, 1989; Curt Smith, Coolidge, 1989.

Randolph Childress, Flint Hill, 1990; Michael Smith, Dunbar, 1990; Victor Page, McKinley, 1994; Keith Bogans, DeMatha, 1999.

Then there are the recent players who might crack the top twenty-five down the road, but for now their basketball stories are still works in progress:

Jeff Green, Northwestern, 2004; Sam Young, Friendly, 2004; Scottie Reynolds, Herndon, 2006; Austin Freeman, DeMatha, 2007; Chris Wright, St. John's, 2007.

A case can be made — and in most cases, was made — for all of the players, who can tell legendary stories. Fact or fiction: Did Curt Smith really jump out of his mother's moving car because he would do anything to avoid taking the SAT? An unforgettable sight was Sam Young doing backflips the length of the Comcast Center court after leading Friendly to a state title. Chris Wright scored more than 2,000 points in his career and was a three-time All-Met, but Austin Freeman was the All-Met Player of the Year their senior season, something the former St. John's coach Paul DeStefano reminds me of every so often.

In short, everyone was considered; this is the best list that could be made. Rest assured, no choice was made to be politically correct.

And while we hope the book will shed some light on legends of the past, we know the barbershop debate always will continue, for in Washington, D.C., this is the never-ending discussion.

25. Lew Luce

Yes, it is true, Lew Luce says. He used to dribble a basketball nearly everywhere he went as a teenager.

And yes, it is true, the three-sport standout at Wilson High during the mid-1950s did have the unusual pregame routine of napping in the locker room.

But wearing pajamas under his clothes to the locker room before games to be more comfortable for his naps? That, Luce says, is legend.

"I'm a different type of person," Luce said with a laugh.

Of course, nothing was too far-fetched for Luce, whether it was success on the football field, basketball court or baseball diamond, or hosting the party of the weekend at his family's home in the Chevy Chase neighborhood of Northwest Washington.

Who else would start his college career with a two-day or two-week (depending on whose version of the story one is to believe) stay at one school before – unbeknownst to his parents – transferring to another school?

Who else would captain the Penn State University freshman football team and, once ready for the spotlight of the varsity, quit school to get married and start a family?

Who else, after three years of trying to find his way academically, could get a tryout with the Washington Redskins and then make the team?

Who else, after taking such a long route to become a professional athlete, would leave halfway through his rookie season, fed up with teammates teasing him while he was injured, according to newspaper reports at the time?

"The Redskins had a hard-line coach named Abe Gibron and he says, 'Luce, every time I talk to you I get convinced your first name is not Lew,'"

3

said Martie Zad, the former sports editor of The Washington Post who was a reporter covering high school sports when Luce was at Wilson. "Because you have a screw loose!"

This was, after all, a guy who was offered a scholarship to play sports at St. John's College High School. But first he had to interview with school officials.

"I lived pretty close to St. John's, so I went over there," Luce said. "Back in the old days, I remember, the priest brother and [basketball coach] Joe [Gallagher] were there. And they asked, 'What does your father think about Catholicism?' Joe said it a couple times. And I told him, 'I don't know, but my father doesn't like Catholics very much.' "

Naturally, a few years after he graduated from a high school other than St. John's, Luce married a Catholic, Mary Lou (not Lew) Gardiner, and they raised their three children as Catholics.

Despite his rather interesting interview, St. John's still would have taken Luce. Gallagher, to this day, calls Luce "the second-best all-around athlete ever from the area," after Jack George.

But in the mid-1950s, one's neighborhood was a galvanizing force. And one of Luce's buddies told him, "Yeah, you go to St. John's, but just don't come back in this neighborhood. You go to Wilson or get out of the neighborhood."

Luce listened. He would be a three-sport star for the Tigers.

As a junior during the 1954-55 school year, after missing five weeks because of a shoulder injury, Luce threw a thirty-yard touchdown pass to John Webster that lifted Wilson a 7-6 victory over Theodore Roosevelt to clinch the Interhigh's West Division title.

That winter, he began his scoring binge on the basketball court. The six-foot, one-inch guard had thirty-two points in a victory over St. Anthony's and twenty-seven in a victory over Landon (one of its players was Donald Dell, who went on to be a highly successful tennis player and sports agent). For the second season in a row, Luce was second among Interhigh scoring leaders, averaging twenty-one points per game. He was named second-team All-Met by The Post.

As a senior, Luce continued to shine in football. He caught a sixty-five-yard touchdown pass with seventeen seconds left to beat the Roosevelt again, 14-9. Against Coolidge, Luce rushed for one hundred thirty-five yards and two touchdowns on six carries and intercepted two passes in a 27-7 victory. He threw two touchdown passes in a 19-13 loss to Cardozo in a game that decided the Interhigh division title.

Luce was named third-team All-Met by The Post, but later won the Joseph T. Sanford Memorial Award, given by the Touchdown Club of Washington to the area's best high school football player.

In basketball, Luce was even more dangerous during the 1955-56 season, scoring forty-seven points in a loss to St. John's and earning first-team All-Met honors.

Luce was a standout in baseball and wanted to run track, too. "But the rules wouldn't let you do two sports at the same time," he told The Post's Alan Goldenbach a few years ago when Goldenbach was writing a story about Sherwood High two-sport standout Deontay Twyman.

At the same time, Luce was known around town for his easy-going attitude and an ability to host seemingly world-class parties. While Washington remained a segregated city, Luce often could be found in Anacostia playing against black opponents. He did not care much about race, willing to go anywhere and do anything. Willie Jones, the high-scoring Dunbar star, remembered borrowing Luce's car to take his date to the prom.

Jones "would come up to my neighborhood to a party and it was fine," Luce said. "And I went down to a party in his neighborhood and it was super. I used to love going down there in summertime."

Yes, Luce was a bit of a free spirit.

"He used to leave the keys in his car in front of his house," said Tom McCloskey, who went to Gonzaga and joined Luce on the 1955-56 All-Met basketball team. "A couple of guys knew this and would take the car home and bring it back in the morning."

But as much as he succeeded on the playing fields, Luce struggled in the classroom. While many in the Wilson senior class of 1956 headed to college, Luce needed a year at Bullis Prep in Silver Spring, Maryland.

"They said if I came to Bullis, I didn't have to pay, that they wanted the publicity," Luce said. "They wanted to use me. I had to play all three sports, which I was going to do anyway, plus I had to board there. They really improved my College Board scores. They used that later to get kids to go there. We had the Number One prep school basketball team in the United States."

After Bullis, Luce accepted a football scholarship to play for the University of Miami, beginning in the fall of 1957.

"I got really p----- off at this guy Andy Gustafson," Luce said.

Gustafson, unfortunately, was the Hurricanes' head coach.

"So I left and came back, and the funny thing was I was afraid to talk to my father," Luce said. "My old football coach [at Wilson] Pete Labukas called [Coach] Rip Engel at Penn State and said I had changed my mind."

A few days later, after Engel had taken Luce at Penn State and the player had arrived in State College, Pennsylvania, Luce phoned his father.

"How are you getting along down at Miami?" inquired Llewellyn Luce, a former football player at Montana State University. He was also a high-powered tax attorney and once defended Al Capone.

Chuckling at the other end of the line, Lew had a quick response: "I'm at Penn State!"

As with many of his teenage and early-twenties endeavors, Luce's tenure in State College was short-lived. Though he had success playing for the freshman team during the 1957 season, Luce still did not have much interest in academics. He left after that season to get married and return to Washington, where he enrolled at D.C. Teachers College, playing football and basketball for two years.

Joe Paterno, Luce said, "was the offensive coordinator [at Penn State] when I came back," Luce said. "I was screwed up at the time."

It was a matter of debate at which sport Luce was best.

At one point, he was going to pursue a career as a center fielder with baseball's Pittsburgh Pirates. He went to play for the Pirates' minor-league team in Kingsport, Tennessee, in the rookie-level Appalachian League. He stayed there three weeks before returning to Washington to reconsider his options, thinking the Pirates would send him to another minor-league team in Wilkes-Barre, Pennsylvania.

"But a guy called and said they were going to send me to South Dakota," Luce said. "My wife said, 'You go ahead, I'm going to stay here with my mother.'"

That was the end of Luce's pro baseball career. And it looked like the end of his professional athletic career.

Lew and Mary Lou had two children and subsequently moved to Fort Lauderdale, Florida, where he enrolled at Broward Community College. Then he got the tryout with the Redskins in the fall of 1961, where he proved his worth as a hungry player eager for any chance.

"The thing is, basketball was probably my favorite sport," Luce said.

But by late October, having played sparingly, Luce left the team and returned to Florida. He played in two games, had three carries for a total of one yard and returned four kickoffs for seventy-seven yards.

"I had a hamstring problem, and I kept going to the doctor and they kept making me go out on the practice team," Luce said. "Back in those days, it was different. . . . It was a big thrill for me to make the team, but it was a bad time for me."

Luce returned to his family in Florida and soon found himself back on the football sideline, but in a much different capacity.

"Then I got the biggest break I ever had, which really got me squared away as far as my education," Luce said. "I was at a banquet with [Florida State University] Coach Bill Peterson. We got to talking and I told him I had not graduated yet. And he said, 'Why don't you come to Tallahassee and help me in spring practice and go back to school?'

"The guy did not know me from the man in the moon, but I took him up on it. Then another guy left the coaching staff. I stayed in school, became a [graduate assistant] and the head freshman coach. I got my master's degree there in education and administration."

One of the Seminoles' assistant coaches was none other than Bobby Bowden.

Luce left Florida State to coach at Brandon [Florida] High for two years, compiling a 16-4 record. In 1966, he returned to Washington to teach and coach football at Wilson, replacing Labukas. From there, he moved to Bullis to coach football, basketball and baseball and be the school's athletic director. Then Luce moved to Montgomery County Public Schools, where he taught at various schools and got into officiating high school and college basketball, working his way up to do games in the Atlantic 10 and Big East conferences.

"I loved that," Luce said. "I loved that more than a lot of things."

Lew and Mary Lou subsequently retired to Apollo Beach, Florida. Lew still had the coaching itch and worked as an assistant high school coach for ten years before giving that up five years ago. Not surprisingly, Luce never told his fellow coaches about his wild career; he simply wanted to be part of the team again.

"Everything has always worked out for me," Luce said.

24. Ed Hummer

At the time, it seemed like the right choice. Ed Hummer was twenty-two years old; he had graduated from Princeton University a few months earlier and subsequently was drafted by the NBA's Boston Celtics.

That September night, in the middle of training camp, he had gone to see Red Auerbach, the Celtics' general manager, seeking assurances he would make the team. Hummer had been admitted to Georgetown University's law school and, if he was not going to make the Celtics' roster that season, he wanted to go to graduate school.

Auerbach, as was his nature, declined to make any guarantees.

So Hummer left Auerbach's stately room in the Lenox Hotel, left Boston and enrolled at Georgetown.

"It was the worst decision I ever made in my life," said Hummer, who starred at Washington-Lee High in Arlington in the early 1960s, then played on the Bill Bradley-led Princeton team that reached the Final Four in 1965 before losing to Michigan.

After all, the odds were in Hummer's favor to make the team.

For starters, Auerbach had a soft spot for players from his adopted hometown. Auerbach had seen Hummer play against St. John's one summer during high school down at the Jelleff Summer League and Hummer had "the best game of my life. We lost something like 37-35 and I wasn't that much of a scorer, but out of the thirty-five, I had thirty-one. Red came up and even spoke to my father after the game."

Auerbach also was fond of players from strong college programs and players who knew their role and did not demand the spotlight. Furthermore, the NBA had just expanded from ten to twelve teams, adding the San Diego Rockets and Seattle SuperSonics. There were roster spots to be had.

Auerbach told Hummer that he was likely to make the squad.

But without a sure thing, Hummer did not want to take any chances.

"So I went back to law school," he said. "Think about it. What I regret is if I had stuck it out, I think I would have made the team. I'm quite sure I never would have played. I think I would have been on the end of the bench. That would have been a thrill -- don't get me wrong.

"Looking at the whole picture – the money, the career thing foregone and delaying law school – at the time I made the stupid decision. After practicing law for ten years, I went back to business school to get my MBA. Looking back, what was I thinking?"

As if Hummer needed further reinforcement that hindsight has twenty-twenty vision, the 1967-68 Celtics won the NBA title. Hummer tried out again the next offseason, but knew he stood little chance as Auerbach was unlikely to make changes near the bottom of the roster. Making matters worse, during tryouts, Hummer tore his Achilles tendon.

Had he played that 1967-68 season, he thinks, he would have had a spot on the 1968-69 team, which also won the NBA title, in Bill Russell's final season as a player.

"That was his nature -- he was always too cautious," former Washington-Lee teammate Lynn Moore said. "Law school was the surer thing."

Instead of wearing around a pair of NBA championship rings, Hummer could look forward to his third year of law school. Hummer does have another pair of championships -- Virginia state titles – that today he can look back on. Back in the early 1960s in Arlington, Ed Hummer was a dominant player, completing his scholastic career by leading the Washington-Lee Generals to thirty-nine consecutive victories.

Born April 10, 1945, in New York City, Ed Hummer was the middle of three children born to Edward Hummer and Lucy Fulwiler. Edward was an FBI special agent and the Hummers moved to Northern Virginia when Ed was one year old, eventually settling in North Arlington. Growing up, Ed enjoyed playing basketball over at the Lyon Village playground; although not a standout, he soon realized he had potential on the court.

"If you needed an indication in life that somebody thinks you might be a decent player, for me it came in seventh grade," Hummer said. "They got some guys together – I wasn't one of them – and they did a draft. All the captains had one hundred points. I was the top draft choice: Someone spent sixty-three points on me. I thought it was ridiculous at the time, but I was tall. There weren't many tall guys at the time."

Hummer would get taller still. He made the Stratford Junior High team but played little as an eighth-grader. Finally, as a ninth-grader – having grown six inches from when he entered Stratford and now standing six-four – Hummer played a significant role as Stratford won the Fairfax County junior high championship.

Although he grew considerably, Hummer's game did not change. Despite being the tallest on the court, he never was a true post player, always more comfortable putting the ball on the floor instead of having his back to the basket. And while many of his peers bounced from one sport to the next, Hummer focused squarely on basketball, although many mistook his serious demeanor for a lack of desire to play.

"Unlike today, you played things seasonally more then," he said. "I was never good at anything but basketball. My mother did one of the nicest things anyone ever did for me. In junior high, I needed permission to go out for football and my mother refused. So I became a basketball player. I would have just gotten my bones crushed in football."

By the time he reached Washington-Lee in the tenth grade, having put in plenty of time practicing, Ed Hummer had blossomed into quite a player on the basketball court. The Generals were a good team that 1960-61 season, finishing 18-5, with three of the losses coming to Wakefield, another Arlington school, which won the Virginia Group A championship. That also was the season that Mount Vernon center Marty Lentz scored seventy-four points in one game.

By his junior season, Hummer was a leader. He grew an inch per year in high school and now stood six-six. He scored a game-high fifteen points in a 53-32 victory over Marion in the quarterfinals of the state tournament. In the semifinals, he had 10 points and 16 rebounds in a 61-49 comeback victory over Andrew Lewis. Finally, Hummer scored a game-high seventeen points and Washington-Lee capped its 23-1 season with a 49-37 victory over Maury in the state final. Hummer was the only junior named to The Washington Post's All-Met, joining John Jones and John Austin of DeMatha, Dave Bing of Spingarn and Sonny Jackson of Blair. (Jackson would ultimately make his mark in baseball, playing 12 years in the major leagues as a shortstop and outfielder.)

"The difference for most high school players comes between their sophomore and junior years," Hummer explained. "It's the time of the greatest physical change, when some guys who look like they are going to be tall stop growing and some don't, and when your skills start developing.

There aren't that many jump shooters in high school, but there are none before then."

Hummer was self-motivated as he tried to improve. But he also got help from Washington-Lee Coach Morris Levin, who during games had a group of female students who would keep a "plus chart" and a "minus chart." The latter included categories such as "failed to meet the ball" and "let his man go baseline."

"You didn't need to know if you violated that last one. You could see immediately as you went to the bench," Hummer said, snapping his fingers. "And you were on the bench for a few minutes."

A former player at the University of Maryland, Levin had a different philosophy than most high school coaches at the time. He insisted on playing man-to-man defense without much help. "You were expected to go over the top of every screen and not switch," Hummer said.

Levin also liked a patient game, one that didn't necessarily let his players shine.

"Mo was a disciple of [University of Maryland Coach] Bud Millikan – you pass the ball one hundred two times before you shoot!" said former Washington Post reporter and editor Martie Zad. "It was so dull. They won all those games 38-24 or some such scores. The guy didn't have a chance to be spectacular."

Consider the moment Hummer was in the school library reading a magazine about high school sports that had a list of the nation's top basketball players, with each player's scoring average. Knowing his average was several points lower than the others on the list, Hummer looked at Levin and asked if his inclusion was a mistake.

"How many on that list won two state championships?" Levin said and walked away.

"There was nothing else you could say," Levin later explained. "He was a complete ballplayer. He could play defense. He could play offense. You could challenge him. He wasn't selfish. Ed Hummer was one of the best ballplayers ever in the state of Virginia."

Lest there be any doubt, Hummer yearned for the chance to play against better opponents, wherever it was, throughout the year.

"When guys got their driver's licenses, we would go anywhere for a game," Hummer said. "The P Street playground in D.C. Fort Belvoir. Anywhere to get good competition. That's something that just doesn't happen anymore. When [his younger son] Ian was at Gonzaga, I asked [Coach] Steve Turner where the players are, what playground do they go to? Steve said, 'I hate to tell you this, Mister Hummer -- those places don't exist anymore.

"The summer between [Ian's] sophomore and junior year, he played something like thirty-plus AAU games and thirty-plus Gonzaga games between the Kenner League and the Rock League. I tell Ian that even with all those games, I guarantee he didn't spend one-third the number of hours I spent on the basketball court in high school. That's just what I did. You went to the playground in the summer and went home for lunch and then back to the playground and back home for dinner.

"Then, when they put in the lights at Lyon Village, you stayed until eleven! I played more games of one-on-one and H-O-R-S-E in one summer than he has played in his whole life. Anybody my age would say the same thing."

After traveling all over during summer, Hummer returned to Washington-Lee for his senior year and Generals started piling on the victories. Hummer scored seven of his eleven points in the first quarter to help build an early lead in a 62-43 victory over Yorktown for the Northern Virginia title. By season's end, Washington-Lee was 26-0 and celebrating another state title. One thing that stood out, looking back, was how reed-thin Hummer was, at six-seven and one hundred eighty-two pounds.

"That was how basketball players looked: Nobody really lifted weights because it was such a pain in the neck. There were no machines then," Hummer said. "I watch some of the classic games, when [Ralph] Sampson was at U-Va., and [Sam] Perkins and [Michael] Jordan were at North Carolina, and it looks like some of these guys are emaciated."

Hummer was recruited by many top programs, but wound up choosing Princeton over Duke and Notre Dame.

"Ivy League basketball then was different … in terms of the players that you could get," Hummer said. "Bradley was the best player in the country his senior year. Other guys on our teams had Division I scholarship offers."

While Ed never made it to the NBA, his younger brother, John did. John followed in his older brother's footsteps, winning one state title at Washington-Lee, playing at Princeton and then spending six years in the NBA.

Ed Hummer's son, Ian, was The Post's All-Met Player of the Year in 2009 and followed his father's footsteps to Princeton, where he was the Ivy League Player of the Year in 2013 and finished as the school's second-leading all-time scorer – to Bradley, of course.

23. Collis Jones

Whether or not Collis Jones was any good at math is irrelevant. He got into games for such little playing time during his freshman year at St. John's College High School that it took little effort to tally up his season total – in seconds.

"I was the last guy on the freshman team -- I counted every second," Jones said. "We would be up twenty-five or thirty points in the second quarter on somebody, but I wouldn't get in until about twenty seconds were left in the game. And [Coach Branson Ferry] would go 'Jones,' Then I'd get in for one play and it was over. I never played a whole minute in a game."

Others might have been tempted to quit the team or put forth less than maximum effort, feeling there was little to gain from the situation.

Jones, however, developed two things during this time in the mid-1960s.

First, he developed a work ethic. One cold, snowy winter night, James Jones was late to pick up his son after practice. Collis took a basketball and began working on a jump shot. Thereafter, he would hide a ball on the top row of bleachers, never thinking he could simply ask the coaches to leave out a ball for him to use.

Jones also dedicated himself toward improving, wanting to show others that he deserved more of a chance.

"Originally I was angry, but then I realized it actually helped me," Jones said. "I can remember [DeMatha Coach] Morgan Wootten talked to Branson Ferry and my father, saying, 'You ought to give Collis a little more time.' He didn't give me that time. But in the long run, it probably helped me because I had a chip on my shoulder for the rest of the time I was there. I had a mission. That helped me academically, too, because your grades had to be in order so that you could play.

"It wasn't like I was a good player, but you usually give guys a shot. I was very raw. But going through that experience, once I did get a chance to play, I knew I was going to do everything in power to continue to play. I'm sure I played more basketball than anybody at St. John's in that time frame. That's what you do. That's how you get better. Then I grew."

That was a key part of the equation, too.

The summer after her son's freshman year, Gertrude Jones wanted the middle of her three children to go on a European trip sponsored by the school. The group would visit six countries in twenty-nine days: England, Belgium, Italy, Germany, Switzerland and France. Airfare, lodging, two meals each day – all for four hundred ninety-nine dollars.

"My mother really believed travel was a lot better education than going to school sometimes," he said.

It was quite a trip for Jones, who had grown accustomed to being in unfamiliar circumstances. The St. John's-Eastern riot at the City Title football game occurred at the end of the 1962 season and the March on Washington took place in August 1963, just before Jones began high school. There were fewer than ten blacks at St. John's at the time, although Jones estimates there were eleven in his freshman class.

"These were some tense times," he said. "The mid- and late sixties, there was a lot going on."

When Jones left for Europe at the beginning of June, he was he was five-foot, ten-inches, nearly able to see eye-to-eye with his father, who was one inch taller.

"When I came back and got off the bus in the St. John's parking lot and my parents are there, I'm looking down on my father and I'm like six-three," Jones said. "I just remember going down to the playground when I got home and all of a sudden it was a whole different thing. I was taller than everybody my age. It came much easier. All I did was play basketball. Even when I was supposed to be doing my chores, I would go play basketball. I'd get in trouble with my father and then the next day, it was the same thing and I wouldn't come back until eleven o'clock at night. It was a different time."

Jones could say goodbye to playing clarinet in the school band, it was determined at a meeting with his parents, Coach Joe Gallagher and the school principal.

"The kicker was, Gallagher told me it was possible I could even get a scholarship to college to play basketball," Collis said. "My mother heard that and she said, 'Really?' I just loved basketball. I had no idea that would happen. I was naïve growing up. In D.C., that's all there was. Once I grew,

I was in a perfect situation because I could play at St. John's. If I was at DeMatha or Mackin, maybe I wouldn't have gotten the chance."

Instead of being buried on the depth chart or written off by one of the area's powerhouse programs, though, Jones now had plenty of playing time and the opportunity to develop. Starting on the junior varsity as a sophomore, he tried to mimic Boston Celtics star center Bill Russell.

"In my head, I was Bill Russell," Jones said. "I tried to block every shot. I tried to get every rebound."

While he had a gentle touch, Jones also was learning how to scowl on the court.

"You're supposed to grab a rebound with two hands," he said. "But [jayvee coach Bobby] Reese taught me to one time go up and snag it with one hand and bring it down and smack it with your other hand right next to the guy's ear! The next time, he's going to be looking for where you are and he's not going for the ball. He's going to make you sure you don't hit him in the ear."

Jones moved up to the varsity for the final game of the season, at La Salle University. He held his own, which helped his confidence, though he remained tentative at times the next season, when he started at center. St. John's beat Mackin by two points in that 1965-66 season, quite an achievement considering the Trojans featured Austin Carr and Tommy Littles.

"I fouled out of that Mackin game; I was battling bigger guys most of the time," Jones said. "Usually it was someone my size or taller, and they weighed more because I was skinny."

Jones had developed into a gym rat, constantly wanting to play and improve. But being from St. John's – not a public school and not one of the established Catholic basketball powers – Jones consistently had to prove himself on the court. The next summer, during the Jelleff League, college coaches started approaching Jones, gauging his interest in their schools.

"Back in my day, you went down to the playground, I didn't ask my father to take me here or there. And there was no negotiation at the playground -- you had to learn to get along," Jones said. "And you didn't have your parents with you. If something happened, you had to talk your way out of it or fight your way out of it. People didn't like me because I went to St. John's."

As a six-seven senior, Jones had worked his way into becoming quite a player. He scored twenty-three points and had nineteen rebounds in a lopsided victory over Landon and led St. John's to a 14-9 record, its only losses to local high school teams coming to DeMatha and Mackin. At season's end, Jones was a first-team All-Met.

"When I made All-Met, I was shocked," Jones said. "I didn't set out that I was going to make All-Met. From the time I made it, I was walking around on a cloud. I had followed basketball religiously. I could tell you all the All-Mets and where everybody went. It was Washington basketball. It made me think of when I was a freshman, watching Mackin playing St. John's, and Austin Carr was starting. I was thinking, 'Where are we going to be in four years? Who are going to be the stars?' It didn't strike me to think of myself. That was a big deal to me."

Said teammate Jorge Garayta: "He was always the hard worker and wasn't the big star. It wasn't until our senior year of high school that he started to get attention."

Soon, Jones knew where he was going to college. Carr already had decided he wanted to play for Notre Dame; he and Jones went to the South Bend, Indiana, campus the same weekend for a visit.

"I had played against him in summer league and during the year, but we didn't speak or anything," Jones said. "Frannie Collins picked both of us up. Austin already had it that he was going to Notre Dame, so he was trying to recruit guys to go with him, so he would be on a good team, which was smart. We really hit it off."

At Notre Dame, Jones still could not find the spotlight; that belonged to Carr.

Consider the night his senior year when Jones scored a career-high forty points at Butler. Carr, naturally, scored fifty.

"They don't mention the eighteen rebounds I had in that game," Jones said. "I was proud of that, but mad I didn't get twenty."

Jones still ranks in Notre Dame's all-time leaders in points (seventeenth, 1,367) and rebounds (eighth, 884).

Selected in the first round of the 1971 NBA draft by the Milwaukee Bucks and in the first round of the American Basketball Association draft by the Dallas Chaparrals, Jones had a decision to make. He also knew he was not going to have a lengthy pro career; his back had been hurting so much that doctors told him he probably would be able to play five more years.

"I'd have played for a dollar in the NBA, just the chance to play," Jones said. "But as it turned out, the offers were so different. It was guaranteed money – four hundred twenty-six thousand versus two hundred fifty thousand."

Baltimore Bullets owner Abe Pollin, bumping into Jones at a dinner to honor Carr, told Jones not to go to the rival ABA because the league was having financial problems. Jones, though, had a flight the next day to Dallas and signed with the Chaps. Jones played four seasons, averaging 8.1 points and 4.7 rebounds, before his back forced him to retire.

He returned to Washington and went to work, first for his father's construction business. Jones sold Pella windows, was director of operations for the National Newspaper Association, then became a financial adviser. When blood clots prevented him from working a desk job, Jones started working as a security guard. He then worked as a special police officer for the U.S. Army Corps of Engineers.

Living in Northeast Washington, Collis and Sharon Jones have four grown children.

"I consider myself a late bloomer," Jones said. "It wasn't like I did that much my junior year. I played freshman, jayvee, two years of varsity. Austin Carr, [DeMatha's] Sid Catlett -- those guys played four years on the varsity. Those guys came into school developed. I was not developed. I was the youngster in the group and they treated me like that, too. But I was hungry to play basketball. I would go anywhere to play basketball."

22. Lawrence Moten

How silly it must have looked to anyone passing by the field on many an afternoon near the intersection of Florida Avenue and North Capitol Street in Northeast Washington in the early 1980s.

There was this boy who just seemed troubled. He was pretending to be a quarterback and a wide receiver and a defender – all at the same time, with nobody else around. Get close enough to hear his crackling voice and you would realize he also was the broadcaster.

"A lot of people didn't understand how I could play football by myself," Lawrence Moten said. "They didn't understand how I would tackle myself. They would look at me and say I'm crazy.

"I would hike the ball to myself and throw it in the air and I would have to run and catch it like a receiver. James Lofton was one of my favorite receivers at the time, so it was, 'Lynn Dickey throws to James Lofton.' I'd act like somebody was tackling me, so I'd fall. I would be out there for at least an hour or two. Sometimes it was raining. I was strange, man."

It was the same way on the basketball court, as Moten often played offense and defense. At the same time. With commentary, of course.

"Playing basketball, Magic [Johnson] was always checking me," he said. "I said I was going to be in the NBA or NFL, so get ready. There was no doubt in my mind at that age. I knew I was going to play in the NFL or NBA."

If only it was that easy.

Yet, for Moten, it seemingly was.

At Archbishop Carroll High, he twice made first-team All-Met in football and basketball. He was the first player in more than a decade to accomplish that feat.

Moten was the All-Met Defensive Player of the Year in football as a senior in 1989 and had plenty of opportunities to play defensive back in college. In fact, many college basketball coaches assumed Moten would play football in college and didn't put much effort into recruiting a player they thought they had no chance to get.

Basketball, though, was the sport Moten chose to pursue.

After a year of prep school and a rejection by University of Maryland as that school coped with the death of Len Bias, Moten starred at Syracuse University. There, the smooth-shooting guard and small forward earned the nickname "Poetry in Motion" as he became the Orangemen's all-time leading scorer and the all-time leading scorer in the Big East Conference. He played three seasons in the NBA.

It was quite a career for the little boy who enjoyed taking the court or hitting the field by himself and used his imagination.

There were plenty of kids in the neighborhood who enjoyed playing – eleven-on-eleven in football, five-on-five in basketball. But there were times not everyone wanted to play, and that included Moten's two younger sisters, who were never into sports. (Two older sisters and an older brother grew up with his father, Lawrence Moten Jr.)

Lawrence Jr. and Lorraine had gone to McKinley Tech, and that school or Dunbar High would have been his neighborhood school had Moten not gone to Carroll.

He first took a visit to DeMatha Catholic High in Hyattsville and met its legendary coach, Morgan Wootten, but he opted to stay closer to home and play for Carroll.

"I got a scholarship to Carroll," Moten said. "It was pretty much a two-handed deal. It was understood that I was going to go there and play both sports. It wasn't a one-sport type of thing. I can remember me and my mother going to meet the Carroll family. I was introduced to both [basketball coach] Carroll [Holmes] and [football coach] Maus Collins."

"You started hearing about Moten before he went to high school," Wootten said. "We definitely wanted him, no question. What an athlete. Just incredible."

It did not take long for Moten to establish himself as one of the city's elite players. Carroll football standout Marvin Graves, a quarterback and defensive back, remembers Moten standing out on the junior varsity football team. Then, in the winter, Moten would have made the Lions' varsity basketball team, but opted to stay on the junior varsity squad.

"Carroll Holmes wanted me to play varsity, but I kind of didn't like the setup. ... I knew I wouldn't play much," Moten said. "That's the only way to get better, to play. I can remember, it's funny, Carroll Holmes being very mad at me for not choosing to play varsity. I can't remember what he said, but I remember his look.

"For maybe a couple weeks, he wouldn't speak to me in the hallways or in class. I think he was a little upset, but as weeks went on and I started playing well on the jayvee and being the leading scorer, hopefully he understood."

Known for his perpetual scowl, the coach had plenty of opportunities to smile over Moten's play during the next three years.

Holmes "was a lunatic," Graves said. "When I look back on it, even during my college days, and look back on what our coaches took us through and the way they coached us and worked us in practice, Carroll Holmes was just hard-nosed.

"He wouldn't be a spokesmodel for a Wheaties box or anything like that. But he was going to bring a parent's son up and under his wing and teach you how to be a man. He wanted to make sure he got the best out of you. He's one of the reasons why I always felt I had a desire to get better and not get complacent with basketball, with football, with life in general."

As a sophomore, Moten started at defensive back and helped Carroll to a 10-1 record on the football field. He then made first-team all-league in the Metro Conference during basketball season.

The star was on his way.

Responsible for recruiting a large swath of the Northeast, Syracuse assistant coach Wayne Morgan always made a point of going to the Jelleff League all-star game each summer. It was there that he first saw Moten.

"He's a sophomore [going into his junior year], and it looks to me like he's the best player I'm seeing in the game," Morgan said. "And I don't think anybody else is seeing that."

Morgan started writing recruiting letters to Moten. In the fall, Moten made The Washington Post's All-Met football team:

Height, reaction time and quickness helped junior grab seven interceptions, returning one for a score . . . good open field tackler . . . fine tight end also, with 65 catches and 10 touchdowns and six two-point conversions for 9-1 metro conference champion Lions . . . good basketball player.

Then he went back to the basketball court and continued to stand out. He had forty-eight points in a 101-100 loss to the host team in the final of the Mount Vernon Holiday Invitational, and twenty-one points and seven rebounds in a 71-50 victory over St. John's.

Morgan made a midseason trip to Carroll to see the Lions play DeMatha. Again, Moten impressed, even though he and Graves combined to miss all thirteen of their three-point attempts. After the game, Morgan made his way downstairs toward the locker rooms and coaches' offices, but was unable to speak with Holmes.

"Carroll Holmes won't even talk to me," Morgan said. "I literally went to the manager, introduced myself, said I really liked what I saw and now I was going to leave. I never talked to the kid, wasn't even sure if he knew I was there."

Morgan called Holmes the next week, hoping to make inroads and gauge whether Moten would have any interest in Syracuse.

"There is no need to come down and recruit the kid," Morgan said Holmes told him. "He's not interested in you or Syracuse. There is no need to call."

"I took him at his word," Morgan said, figuring there were plenty of other prospects to chase.

Moten scored twenty-three points in a 74-69 victory over top-ranked Flint Hill in the final of the St. James Invitational, then scored a game-high twenty-two points as the Lions rallied to beat the Gonzaga Eagles, 83-81, in a playoff for the Metro Conference second-half title.

Carroll then advanced to its first City Title Game in 29 years, only to lose to Dunbar as Donald Ford made a thirty-five foot shot at the buzzer – a shot that still stings Moten.

"When it went in and the buzzer went off, it was like somebody hit me with a sledgehammer," Moten said. "I was laying on the ground, with my eyes closed. You could feel the tramples of people celebrating. And my mother and brother picked me up. I was so sick."

The feeling got worse.

Moten was watching the local television news that night when the highlights came on. In a postgame interview, Ford had the presence of mind to do what other champions of the time said to the cameras: 'I'm going to Disney World."

"I shut off the TV and jumped in my bed," Moten said. "That was a quote I'll never forget."

"People still talk about that game to this day, how that was one of the best City Title games ever in this area," said Graves. "Just last week some guys were talking about it. We had a Cinderella season going on and when Donald Ford hit that shot, it took the air out of it. We felt we had the better team. We took them a little light."

The season, however, was a success, as Moten was selected an All-Met for the second time that season:

First junior to be selected to first team All-Met football and basketball teams in two decades . . . fine perimeter shooter who averaged three three-pointers per game with a season high of eight against DeMatha . . . averaged 24.4 points with a season-high 48 versus Mount Vernon . . . also had 10.1 rebounds and four steals in leading Lions to first Metro Conference championship in 29 years.

A few weeks later, the phone rang in the Syracuse University men's basketball office. Morgan was surprised when a secretary told him Lawrence Moten was on the line.

"Are you guys interested in me?" Moten asked Morgan in his high-pitched voice. "I know you came and saw me play once."

Morgan related his conversation with Holmes.

"No, that's not true," Moten said.

The Orangemen were back in pursuit of Moten, but there would be a few twists before he got to Syracuse.

As a senior during the 1989-1990 school year, Moten continued to excel. Although his mother encouraged him to skip the football season and focus on basketball, he again was a two-sport All-Met. The writeup from the football team pretty much summed things up:

The Washington Post Defensive Player of the Year . . . sure-handed receiver who intercepted an astounding 13 passes from safety position . . . returned one 101 yards for a touchdowns against St. John's . . . had 55 receptions, including 13 for touchdowns.

In basketball, Moten was just as tough. He scored thirty points in an 87-80 victory over Philadelphia Roman Catholic in the semifinals of the Kenner Tournament, then scored twenty-five in the final as Carroll overcame a fifteen-point deficit to beat Dunbar, 85-81, in the final as teammate Charles Harrison scored thirty-four points.

Made All-Met in both basketball and football in junior and senior year . . . superior athletic ability enabled him to average 28.3 points, 10.1 rebounds for No. 11 Lions . . . speed and strength made him a force on both ends of the court, with ability to score inside and outside ... had a one-game season-high of 42 points.

Moten scored thirteen points in the local squad's Capital Classic victory in April. The next month, Moten signed a National Letter-of-Intent to play for Syracuse, choosing the Orangemen over Georgetown and Seton Hall.

But low scores on the Scholastic Assessment Test meant that Moten would not be eligible for an athletic scholarship as a freshman at Syracuse.

He enrolled at New Hampton Prep in New Hampshire, with the intent of improving his academic resume and enrolling at Syracuse in the fall of 1991.

During that season, however, Syracuse was under NCAA investigation for alleged transgressions. Moten started to think that maybe he should go to a different college. Gary Williams, in his first season at the University of Maryland, lured Moten to sign with the Terrapins. Ultimately, though, Moten and top prospect Donyell Marshall were denied admission.

It was a devastating blow for Maryland and difficult for Moten as well, who went back to Syracuse.

"They were coming off the Bob Wade era and trying to revamp things," Moten said. "To this day, there is no doubt in my mind it was a blessing in disguise the way it happened. Who knows -- I might have been close to home with family and friends wanting this or that. At Syracuse, the only person I knew was Marvin Graves."

Folks in Syracuse soon knew plenty about Moten, as the six-foot, five-inch swing man quickly moved into the starting lineup. Four years later, he left as the school's all-time leading scorer, with 2,334 points, and as the all-time leading scorer in Big East conference play, with 1,405 points. For his career, Moten averaged 19.3 points and was a model of consistency, scoring in double figures in one hundred eighteen of one hundred twenty-one games. Not since Dave Bing in the 1960s had the same player led the Orangemen in scoring in three consecutive seasons.

"He's got the best body control," Morgan said. "That's what separates Lawrence from everybody. He has complete muscular control. Whatever space to the rim you let him fit into, he can do it."

Taken by the Vancouver Grizzlies in the second round of the 1995 NBA draft, Moten played for the team for two seasons and joined the Washington Wizards for the 1997-98 season. He averaged 6.3 points per game during his NBA career. He then played overseas and in the minor leagues, and was the vice president of player development for the minor league Maryland Nighthawks.

Moten remained in the Washington area, teaching physical education in Prince George's County before a recent stint coaching the Rochester RazorSharks to the Premier Basketball League championship in 2014. He and his wife have two daughters, Lawrencia and Leilani.

21. Stan Kernan

Stan Kernan never was awed by his surroundings.

First, the kid they all called "Snookie" was the ringleader of McKinley Tech's "Fabulous Five," which strung together three consecutive city championships in the early 1950s.

Then he went into the Navy, made the all-service team and earned an invitation to the 1956 U.S. Olympic trials. There, in Kansas City with the likes of Bill Russell and K.C. Jones, he was the only player yet to play college basketball.

After listening to recruiting pitches from such legendary coaches as Adolph Rupp of Kentucky and Everett Case of North Carolina State, Kernan went on to star at McNeese State University. He left college with one year of eligibility remaining to play for the Akron Goodyear Wingfoots in the National Industrial Basketball League, then had a second run at making the Olympic team. The 1960 Olympic trials in Denver included Oscar Robertson and Jerry West.

While those experiences might leave even the most ho-hum basketball player a bit starry-eyed, it was just basketball to the six-foot, one-inch guard who grew up in an apartment near the intersection of First Street and Rhode Island Avenue in Northwest Washington.

"I really didn't realize what was going on -- nobody told me anything," Kernan said. "Even at the Olympic trials, I probably didn't realize what it was. I knew it was practicing and playing. We didn't have any guidance in high school from coaches at all. Nobody on that team got to school, got to college. You don't have the scouts like they do now and the all-star games. Really, we didn't get the exposure back in those days."

Give some notice, though, and Kernan can produce the scrapbooks and other memorabilia that show indeed he was one of the Washington area's first basketball stars.

Kernan was not just a basketball player. He was a running back on the McKinley football team in the fall. In the spring, he ran track, claiming a city championship in the 100-yard dash.

But he was best at basketball, a sport he picked up by chance one day as a youngster when he became bored with the neighborhood games of hide-and-seek and kickball.

"One day I said, 'I'm going to go up to the playground,'" Kernan said. "So I went up by myself and some guys were playing basketball. I didn't know how to play. But I could jump, so they let me play with them. I'd jump, get the rebound and pass the ball to them."

Pretty soon, Kernan was playing at the Number 12 Boys' Club. Then he moved on to Langley Junior High, where the nucleus of the Fabulous Five was formed.

"We all played together; I never even scored much back then," Kernan said. "We just kept developing. One thing we did was play at Edgewood playground. That's where Jack [George] played. It was a dirt court. That's where I really learned to play."

Why were the city's best youth players going to a dirt court? Nobody seemed to know.

"Get out of there and you had mud up to your knees," Kernan said. "I imagine [the ball bounced], I don't remember. But you'd go home and be muddy, all dirty."

Kernan also benefited from tutelage from members of the old Washington Capitols, who played in the Basketball Association of America, which later merged with another league to form the National Basketball Association. The Capitols' coach, Red Auerbach, had a summer job running the pool at the Langley playground, and some of his players occasionally stopped by.

"So they helped out," Kernan said, remembering forward Johnny Norlander teaching him a bit. "Back when I was playing with Goodyear, he came and talked to me one time when I was playing in Denver. 'You sure remember me. Amazing.'"

In the fall of 1949, Kernan and his buddies arrived at McKinley for their sophomore year of high school. There, Coach Dutch Usilaner had the Trainers playing a fast-break brand of basketball that was rarely seen.

Bill Breen was the outside shooter. Frank Sullivan, the tallest starter at six-three, played center. Joe Caw and Babe Marshall also played in the backcourt.

"We didn't really have positions, though," Kernan said. "You just went where you went. We never had [plays]. As a coach, I didn't teach plays, but just where you're supposed to go. We didn't even have that. All we did was run: Get down the court as fast as you can and whoever has the best shot, shoots."

Kernan was the fastest of the bunch and also the designated scorer, with a rarely-seen jump shot in an era when most players used a set shot.

"I really believe he shot a better jump shot [during high school] than he did later on," Sullivan said. "Later on, he seemed to change when he was in the Navy. He sort of put the ball differently in his hand. He still scored, though. Anytime you wanted points, give it to Snookie. … He was a prolific scorer."

Said Caw: "He was always the guy we could depend on. If you needed a basket, he could get a basket for you."

Exactly where did that jump shot come from? Even Snookie – a nickname coined by his mother when he was a child -- is not sure.

"I keep thinking I watched somebody on television, but I don't know whether it's true or not," he said. "Nowadays, I probably would have charged so many times I'd have fouled out of the game. But back then, you could just run over the person."

As a junior, Kernan led McKinley against Eastern for the Interhigh football championship. Both teams were unbeaten. That day's Washington Post declared the Trainers six-and-a-halfpoint favorites, but the Ramblers won, 20-6.

In basketball season, though, McKinley successfully defended its league title, as Kernan scored twenty-five points and Breen had twenty-three in a 73-59 victory over Coolidge before one thousand fans at the old Uline Arena. It was the first time in ten years that an Interhigh team had gone undefeated in the league's regular season play and won the postseason tournament.

After a 62-34 victory over Coolidge before four thousand at Ritchie Coliseum in the All-Metropolitan Tournament, Kernan was named to The Post's All-Metro team along with Player of the Year Bob Kessler from George Washington, Gerry LeCompte of Gonzaga, Bob Reese of St. John's and Lou Snouffer of Western.

The next summer, however, Kernan faced his biggest challenge yet at McKinley.

Before the school year, the Kernans had moved to suburban Prince George's County. Now residents of Maryland, Stan and his younger sister, Shirley, were supposed to attend school there instead of in the District.

"One day I came to school and they said, 'You can't go to school here. You have to go Bladensburg,'" Kernan said.

That posed a problem. While Bladensburg Coach Merle Duvall phoned Kernan to try to talk the player into enrolling at the school and joining the team, Kernan not only did not want to leave McKinley, he was worried about potentially having to play against McKinley in the Evening Star tournament.

"I had been playing with these guys all my life," Kernan said.

Eventually, Kernan joined another select club: Students who paid their way to attend a D.C. public school.

"I don't know who paid the money," Kernan said. "Everybody said it was my father, but I doubt it was."

Getting from Rogers Heights in East Riverdale to McKinley could be a challenge.

"I'd either walk, hitchhike or get a ride," Kernan said. "That's why I was in shape, I think. I didn't drive or have a car. And the buses only ran out there at certain times. I used to walk at midnight going home after being out with the guys. And if I saw something, I could run. Couldn't catch me. I'd walk down them dark roads and if something moved, I'd take off."

Those, of course, were different days. It wasn't often that Snookie Kernan had to take off running.

As a senior at McKinley, Kernan was a second-team All-Interhigh running back, then was named captain of The Post's All-Metropolitan team, with Kessler, Reese, Breen and guard Jerry Eckholm of Priory also named to the first team. He capped his McKinley career with a tap-in at the buzzer to beat George Washington and was carried off the court.

The one opponent Kernan never played against in high school was Elgin Baylor, who was at Spingarn. Because of segregation, the only time they faced each other was on the playground.

"I wish we could have" played during the high school season, Kernan said. In the summer, "Elgin would bring his group and we'd take our high school team and play. People would be all over the place. It wasn't a game like today where they fight or argue. You just played. Respect for each other, I think it was."

After Kernan graduated from McKinley in 1952, with the Korean War in full swing, his next stop was with the Navy. Deployed to a destroyer, Kernan would play whenever the ship was in port and he had an opportunity.

On one occasion, Kernan played with a lieutenant who was impressed and recommended getting him a tryout for the fleet's team in Norfolk. By the time he arrived, however, the season had started. Kernan sat for two weeks until the coach was fired and a new coach gave him an opportunity.

"I made all-Navy," Kernan said.

From there, he made the all-service team, which went to the Olympic trials along with two teams from the National Industrial Basketball League and a college all-star team.

"They took care of me because I wasn't a college player, especially Don Lange from Navy," Kernan said. "They were good to me because I was just a kid, a high school kid. They all had experience and had been famous or whatever. Nobody knew who I was. But they treated me good."

It was there, in Kansas City, that Kernan somehow became a college prospect, as coaches apparently learned he was the only player who had yet to start his eligibility.

"Adolph Rupp and Everett Case came to my room," Kernan said. "I had all these people coming to my room and asking me to go to college. I was just getting ready to get out of the service then."

One of the players on the college all-stars was Bill Reigel, a small-college all-American from McNeese State. His coach, Ralph Ward, came to Kansas City to watch but ended up with a few new players after he met Kernan.

"I'd like to come down and visit," Kernan told Ward. "But I've got two buddies who are good basketball players and haven't gone to college yet. Would you take them, too?"

"He offered to take those two guys with me so I said, 'Okay, I'll go.' Nobody else would have offered that, I'm sure."

Breen ended up staying at McNeese, while Gonzaga grad Gerry LeCompte – often mistaken as a McKinley student and alumnus because he always was around -- never made it into a game.

"He didn't like it," Breen said. "He said it was a little hick town."

Not that Kernan and Breen were instantly sold on their new school tucked away in southwestern Louisiana.

"We both came down here and stayed two weeks and really didn't like it, and went back to D.C.," Breen said. "It was kind of a small town, though it's grown now. But we got back up there, and the athletic director was up there and called me at the house and wanted to know if I could get ahold of Snookie and go up to the Willard Hotel to see if we could go back.

"Coach Ward wanted another try, and he'd take us out deep sea fishing and water skiing. So we turned around and went back down there. And we stayed.

"Snookie was going to buy a car and I was going to buy a car, and [Ward] took us to the Ford dealership and got us a good deal. He got us a good discount. We paid for it. We were going to school on the GI Bill."

The NCAA might be interested in such transactions now, but in the late 1950s no one knew any better.

Settled in Louisiana, Kernan excelled at McNeese State, earning all-American honors himself. But since the state of Louisiana prohibited the Cowboys from playing against teams with black players in the season-ending NAIA tournament, the McNeese players joined a local Amateur Athletic Union team. After Kernan's junior year, they advanced to the AAU national tournament in Denver.

"We beat Goodyear, I scored 20-some points and they gave me a call and said, 'Would you come play for Goodyear?'" Kernan said.

By that point, Stan and his wife, Louise, had one child. The offer was a good one: Work for Goodyear and learn the tire business while playing for the company team.

It was too good to pass up and Kernan had fun, traveling the nation to play in the NIBL and training all over the factory when he was back in Akron.

"You would go to classes, different parts of the factories, the company," Kernan said. "After one year, you would have gone into whatever field you would have gone into. It was like school. I actually worked in the factory – making tires, stacking tires, working in the office. But I knew I wasn't going to work in the factory. I didn't like that."

After a year in Akron, though, Kernan was on the move again. The NIBL folded and Kernan – technically still an amateur because he was paid by Goodyear as an employee, not as a basketball player – went back for his final year of eligibility at McNeese.

After graduation, the Kernans moved back to Maryland, where they discussed whether Stan should pursue a professional basketball career.

"I talked with the Washington team, but they only offered five thousand dollars," Kernan said. "I had three kids then and I had to get a job. I was no youngster. I had spent four years in the service. So I got a job."

Kernan first taught at a junior high school. When Parkdale High opened in 1968, Kernan was its first boys' basketball coach, guiding the Panthers for 10 seasons and winning state titles in 1971 and 1976.

"But they weren't paying anything and it was time-consuming, I had four children at home," Kernan said. "The girls played during the daytime."

So Kernan switched to coaching girls' basketball. He was an assistant coach at first, helping the Panthers win a state title in 1978. He soon became the head coach and became the first coach in Maryland history to win boys' and girls' state championships, leading Parkdale to the 1981 state title.

"Coaching is hard; playing is easy, I think," Kernan said. "It was a hard job. You've got to be a disciplinarian, but you've got to be friendly and have a relationship with the kids and still be the boss."

Kernan retired from Parkdale in 1988, the same year he was inducted into the Louisiana Basketball Hall of Fame. (In 1983, he had been inducted into the McNeese Athletics Hall of Fame.) After one year of traveling across the nation with Louise, they settled into the Charles Town, West Virginia, home they once built for vacations. He spent a few years as an assistant coach at nearby Jefferson High, but now hits the court only to get in a few shots at a nearby Gold's Gym.

Occasionally, members of the Fabulous Five reunite to tell stories about their glory days.

"It's a team, a bunch of guys that came together," Kernan said. "Like [Louise] says, somebody was watching out for me. I never did anything on my own. It just seemed to happen."

20. Stacy Robinson

As the rest of his teammates hit the floor for pregame warm-ups, basketball star Stacy Robinson usually would find an excuse not to join them.

"Man, I've got to throw up."

"I've got a stomach virus."

"I've got to go to the bathroom."

Then he would sneak away. Back to the locker room. A bathroom. Under the bleachers. Anywhere he could be alone for a few moments to get high.

"I wouldn't come on the floor unless I was good, high and ready to perform," said Robinson, who began high school at Fairmont Heights in 1972, next went to Crossland and completed his eligibility at Dunbar in 1975. "It was like being at a rock concert when the big lights come on. Once I got it in me, I was good and ready. Let the show begin."

And what a show it was, starting from when Robinson was a youngster, ruling local basketball leagues on teams coached by Earl Davis.

The flashy guard had everything in his bag of tricks. He could score. He could pass. And he did it all with considerable flash, with plenty of people paying attention.

Consider a feature story written by The Washington Post's Thomas Boswell during Robinson's senior year of high school. It described Robinson as "a star since 10, center of controversy since 11 and recruited since 12."

At thirteen years old, Robinson and his teammates were given championship trophies to quit a summer league midseason because they were winning every game so easily.

But as Robinson got older, getting on the court became harder.

He was academically ineligible to play basketball as an eighth-grader. The next year, playing at Thomas Pullen Junior High after his family moved to Hillcrest Heights, Maryland, Robinson's coach was Taft Hickman, who went on to a lengthy, successful career. It was there that Robinson first got on the radar of others, with St. Anthony's High Coach John Thompson – who a few years later would take over at Georgetown University – coming to see him.

"I walked into the gym and saw him during warmup and my eyes lit up," Robinson said. "I wondered who he was there to see, me or somebody else. I had like thirty-four points that game. He didn't say that much to me. He just let me know he was there."

That night, Robert Robinson had a talk with the oldest of his five children.

"You know what this means? You're being watched now," the elder Robinson said, hoping this might motivate Stacy. "You have to get in the classroom and apply yourself."

It was a message that Stacy would hear often over the next few years. But yet, regardless of who was doing the talking, it never sank in.

"Going to class wasn't one of my greatest things; I wasn't a guy you could find in the classroom very much," Robinson said. "I would be in the hallways, doing things I shouldn't be doing. But I loved the game of basketball."

It was at Pullen, Stacy said, that he began using drugs.

"I was sniffing glue at first, then after that came the hard stuff," he said. "Cocaine. Heroin. Every chance I could get. There wasn't a day that went by that I didn't go looking for it. I had to have it. When I played [high], I was in my comfort zone. Nobody could do nothing with me on the court."

Robert Robinson wanted Stacy to attend a Catholic high school. He can't remember whether DeMatha Coach Morgan Wootten ever came to see Stacy, though that would have been his first choice. Stacy did not do well on the entrance exams to St. Anthony's and did not get into school there.

"He really didn't get the education he needed in the public schools," Robert Robinson said. "I hate it to this day I didn't get him into a Catholic school back then."

Wootten said he was interested in recruiting Stacy Robinson, but that Robert Robinson preferred his son to play for a black coach.

"Why should he play for you and make a white coach better?" Wootten remembered being told by Robert Robinson. "Why shouldn't he go to play for a black coach and make him better?"

Several Prince George's public school coaches were interested in Robinson.

He considered Bladensburg High, but then-coach Roy Henderson did not make a terrific first impression.

"He said I was a hot dog, that I had a little too much mustard with me," Robinson said. "He didn't like my behind-the-back passes, my no-look passes. He said, 'You'll have to tone that down if you come here.' So I knew I wasn't going to Bladensburg."

The Mustangs were just fine without Robinson; they won the Maryland AA state title the next March. Robinson also considered Central High, but did not like the Falcons' preference to play at a slow pace.

So Robinson enrolled at Fairmont Heights, where he remembers debuting with thirty-five points against Gwynn Park -- and saw Darrel Matthews pour in forty-one for the Yellow Jackets.

"He welcomed me to the high school game," Robinson said. "Another game, we played Bladensburg and [future North Carolina recruit] Bruce Buckley. He destroyed us -- I think he had thirty-nine."

Fairmont Heights was just a pit stop for Robinson. Hornets Coach Ralph Paden, frustrated with Robinson's proclivity to miss practice, took him out of the starting lineup and Robinson quickly became frustrated. He transferred to Crossland, where he was reunited with many of his teammates from Pullen.

"He was surrounded by a whole lot of people who thought he couldn't do anything wrong," Paden said. "But he was still a kid. I was trying to teach him the right thing to do. They were just interested in his basketball skills. … I saw him years after that and he said, 'Coach, I wish I had listened to you. You're the only one to say no to me.' "

On the court at Crossland, Robinson continued his high-scoring ways. He scored thirty-two points in a 70-68 loss to City College of Baltimore and enjoyed a successful season. At year's end, he was named to the Prince George's ABC all-league team.

The next year, as a junior, Robinson again proved his mettle on the court. In one game, he scored twenty of his twenty-six points in the second half to lead Crossland past defending state champion Bladensburg, 82-70. In the Maryland AA-II region final, Robinson scored a game-high twenty-eight points in a 63-57 victory over Suitland. The Cavaliers advanced to the Maryland AA tournament semifinals for the first time before losing to Parkville of Baltimore County, 92-73. Crossland finished 15-7.

After the season, Davis hosted an all-star game at Suitland High, with a team of seniors from high schools in Maryland playing their counterparts from the District. But the Maryland team, Robinson said, had only four players show up.

"I was sitting in the bleachers and one of the coaches asked me if I wanted to play," Robinson said. "Every college coach in the country was there. Norm Sloan [of North Carolina State], Tates Locke [of Clemson], Lefty [Driesell of Maryland], Coach Thompson may have been there, Bobby Cremins [then an assistant at South Carolina], Jerry Tarkanian [of Nevada-Las Vegas]. Hell yeah, I wanted to play in the all-star game, knowing I would be ineligible the next year at Crossland. I had forty-three points."

Subsequenly ruled ineligible to play anywhere in Maryland because such all-star games are only for graduating seniors, Robinson was on the hunt for another school. He decided to enroll at a District public school, eventually deciding between recruiting pitches from Dunbar's Joe Dean Davidson and Eastern's A.B. Williamson.

"Eastern had Turk Tillman; I could go play with Turk or Dunbar -- they had a young guy coming out of junior high school named Craig Shelton," Robinson said. "We played in a summer league game at Kelly Miller. I didn't know who he was before, but this young man got every rebound that came off."

"Who is that?" Robinson asked Davidson.

"That's Craig Shelton," Davidson replied. Shelton had yet to earn the nickname "Big Sky."

"Where's he going to school?" Robinson followed up.

"Dunbar."

"That's where I want to go then," Robinson decided.

Thus, Stacy Robinson joined another select group: those who paid tuition to attend a D.C. public school.

Tuition was three hundred sixty-five dollars per semester.

It was that same summer that Robinson met DeMatha guard Pete Strickland at a Five-Star Basketball Camp. Robinson enjoyed Strickland's guitar-playing Elvis Presley skits; Strickland liked Robinson's ability to do whatever he wanted on the court.

"There was an effortlessness to his game – a stride, an ease, longer that most guards," said Strickland, who went into coaching after his playing career was over. "He was one of the best in my era in terms of being able to score."

At Dunbar, while the soft-spoken Davidson was viewed as a disciplinarian – often locking the gymnasium doors during practice – Robinson did not change. Sometimes he went to school, other times he would hang out on the streets and skip class, which usually meant missing playing time.

"I was a high school all-American: My classwork was being done for me, my books were being carried," Robinson said. "I really wasn't a 'big-head' type of guy, where I thought I was better than everyone, but I was a game player. When I came to practice, I was like, 'I'm here today, let's get to the big show, let's get to the lights and put that red and black on for Dunbar.' "

The Crimson Tide had a sensational squad, and the addition of Robinson and Shelton only made them even tougher. They joined forward Joe Thweatt, guard Emmett Henderson and the Duren brothers, Lonnie and John, who was better known by his nickname, "Bay Bay."

Steve Robinson, two years younger than his older brother, had several talks with him, trying to persuade Stacy to take his schoolwork more seriously, avoid drugs and get on track for college. Like everyone else who brought up the subject, he did not find much success.

"C'mon, Stay, you've got to cut this out," Steve Robinson would say. "You've got everybody in he country recruiting you. You just got letters today from Marquette, Louisville, Kentucky. You need to clean yourself up."

"Man, I've got this," was Stacy Robinson's stock reply.

"But all along I was a mess," he says now, adding that getting the drugs was easy.

"I was an all-American, I was headed to the NBA," he said. "It was, 'Here, Stacy, here you go, great game, I'll see you next week.' Or, 'I bet him you wouldn't get forty for an ounce of coke.' It was mad."

"I didn't see him do it, but I could tell he was high when he was playing," Steve Robinson said. "I just could tell by the way he was acting before a game. He wouldn't really even warm up. He would be sitting on the bench staring. Once they threw that ball in the air, it was like another switch was clicked on. I've never seen anything like it."

Robinson missed the season's first two games because of "injuries," then had twenty-eight points and nine assists in his debut, a 74-68 victory over Archbishop Carroll. Against top-ranked Eastern, Robinson sat out the first six minutes of the fourth quarter and entered with Dunbar trailing, 70-69. He responded with two baskets, an assist and a key steal in a 77-73 victory that boosted the Crimson Tide to The Washington Post's Number One ranking. Eastern played the game under protest because of the crowded conditions, with 2,000 fans packed into Spingarn's gym for the game.

Late in the season, Dunbar beat New York's top-ranked team, Long Island Lutheran, as Thweatt scored twenty-five points and Robinson had seventeen.

The Crimson Tide lost to Eastern, 75-70, in a 1-vs.-2 showdown in the Interhigh tournament championship. And they lost to DeMatha, 67-62, in the City Title Game as Robinson shot three of twelve from the field and scored just six points. Dunbar did exact some payback against DeMatha with a 75-52 victory in the Knights of Columbus Tournament final.

Robinson and Thweatt made The Post's All-Met team, along with Eastern's Tillman and DeMatha junior Hawkeye Whitney.

And that was it for Robinson's high school career. Literally.

"I didn't graduate, I ended up getting a GED," Robinson said. "After basketball season was over with, I was done. I didn't come to Dunbar to go to school. I came to Dunbar to play basketball. Basketball season was over. There was no more reason for me to go to school."

Said Thweatt: "Stacy was so far advanced as far as the ball was concerned, he got bored a lot. Just as an example, we were practicing for the city championship against DeMatha . . . and there were people there from pro teams that was interested in Stacy. There was a lot going on. It was hard for him to concentrate a lot. . . . You could say being a high school sports star wasn't easy for him.

"They definitely catered to him; they would do whatever he wanted. Whatever he wanted to be, it was the Stacy Robinson show. Whatever he wanted to do, whenever. It was everywhere he went. . . . In the Capital Classic, Dorian Dent was going to jump center against [seven-footer] Bill Cartwright. Stacy told him to back up; he was going to do it."

It was a challenging time for Robinson, who also had two children born during his senior year at Dunbar, Kishea Weaver and Stacy Robinson Jr. (Stacy Jr. was an All-Met basketball player at DuVal as a junior in 1991, but was academically ineligible as a senior and never followed through on a commitment to play at Maryland.)

The next fall, Robinson headed to Vincennes University, a two-year Indiana junior college. He didn't go to class and didn't last the season; he does not appear on the Trailblazers' all-time list of players.

"This is not a vacation," assistant coach Kenny Gray told him.

Then came a three-game stop at Barber-Scotia College in Concord, North Carolina.

In the fall of 1976, Robinson attended Delgado Community College in New Orleans, where he earned his graduate-equivalency degree but never stepped foot on the basketball court.

"We didn't have a gym," Robinson said. "I was coming to school one day and saw some guys outside practicing. Is that our team out there? We're in college, playing outside? I caught the first plane home, left all my clothes and stuff."

He ended up playing that year at Laurinburg Institute, a prep school in Laurinburg, North Carolina. After a year away from school, "in the street," Robinson followed Parkdale High's Chick Lyles to Niagara County Community College outside Buffalo. He stayed there the next summer but didn't go back to school.

"I got to drugging again," he said.

He tagged along with another player from that area to Texas A&I University but never became eligible to play there.

"That was my last run," Robinson said. "I was done with it."

Said former Georgetown University coach Craig Esherick, a former standout at Springbrook High in Silver Spring: "He's one of the best players we've ever had in the area who didn't do anything in college. People not from the area think of guys who went on to play in college or went on to play in the pros. The two players guys haven't heard of are Stacy Robinson and Curt Smith."

Robinson returned to Washington, where he worked several jobs, never staying long in one position. He laid carpet and was as a porter at the Greyhound bus terminal, among other things. All the while, he would see former teammates and opponents succeeding on the court and remember how he had "destroyed them."

Finally, several years ago, as his mother, Barbara, became seriously ill, Robinson promised her that "I would get clean and do the right thing." He changed his leisure habits and started attending Narcotics Anonymous-Alcoholics Anonymous meetings. He said he has been clean since and maintained his first steady job, cleaning offices at Amtrak's Union Station offices.

"My whole high school career, it was great, but I cheated the game because I got hooked on narcotics," Robinson said. "I got to fooling around, dibbling and dabbling. I caught a drug habit in high school but I still played ball. . . . I didn't open up to anybody for help back then because I didn't want to let my parents down. I didn't want to let them know I was using drugs. That was totally unacceptable in my house.

"So many cats that come through this city, all they want to talk about is basketball. I didn't accomplish anything. I just recently got my first job at 50-some years old due to me not doing the right things.

"I just hope it reaches one of y'all and you pass it on to somebody else. A lot of people come back and don't talk to kids about how not to make it. They talk about how you can make it.

"Well, this is how you end up when you don't make it. You have no money in your pocket, you have no job, you're asking for handouts and nobody wants to be bothered with you. I think more athletes should talk about the bad points than 'Hey, I have a house in Potomac, Maryland. I have five cars.' Some of these kids don't have bicycles or skates and you come into the gym with big jewelry on now. It's got to change."

19. Ernie Cage

Turn back the clock fifty-five years and try to picture the undistinguished, all-boys Catholic school just off U.S. 1 in Hyattsville, Maryland.

DeMatha Catholic High was still in its infancy, less than ten years old, with maybe 150 students. The Stags had not won a league title in any sport. Morgan Wootten would not be hired for another year. Archbishop Carroll, St. John's and Gonzaga made up Division I in the Metropolitan Catholic League; all other schools were relegated to second-tier status.

The Washington Post's Thomas Boswell, then a rookie reporter before embarking on a distinguished career as a columnist, fifteen years later would write that before Wootten arrived, "DeMatha was probably the most unruly Catholic high school in the Washington area."

The school, however, had a terrific building block in place.

He was a teenager with a flat-top haircut and, wow, could he shoot.

One year later, as Wootten considered an offer to become the DeMatha basketball coach, his good friend Frank Gilmore immediately recognized one of the job's benefits: "They have a great one," Gilmore told Wootten.

It would be a bit much to say that Ernie Cage propelled Morgan Wootten toward becoming a Hall of Fame coach. But everyone agrees: The high-scoring Cage put DeMatha on the athletic landscape and jump-started the Stags toward becoming a sports powerhouse.

In three seasons, Cage scored 2,038 points and earned all-American honors. He was named All-Met each year – third team as a sophomore, second team as a junior and first team as a senior, at a time when The Post included just five players on each squad.

Not all his contributions were on the basketball court – or the baseball field, where he was an excellent pitcher. Ernie Cage also helped Wootten become a master recruiter. Other than Gonzaga, the rest of the Catholic schools eventually turned to co-education, admitting girls to the student body, to maintain enrollment and stay in business. DeMatha, however, started to grow.

"Ernie, more than anybody, became the magnet," Wootten said. "He made it real easy [to recruit]. If a kid came out to visit us, he wanted to meet Ernie.

"I think he definitely put a stamp down. If there was a sport a school was known for, he made it DeMatha and basketball. I don't want to say he made it a basketball school, because we developed great teams in other sports. But early on, it was Ernie who put DeMatha on the map. … We had a lot of young kids around him and they were good athletes and did a good job, but there was only one Ernie Cage. He was obviously the best player in the city at the time. A legitimate high school all-American, no question."

Said Cage's former teammate, Ben Spotts: "We were still the little guy on the block back then. Kids wanted to go where you could win. And Morgan was very charismatic in those days. We liked to say he could sell ice to Eskimos."

The original Eskimo was the six-foot, three-inch Cage. The son of a District of Columbia policeman, Cage attended Bladensburg Junior High and played CYO ball for St. James of Mount Rainier. His exploits began making The Post's sports pages even before he got to high school as he began setting scoring records.

As a sophomore in 1955-56, he was third-team All-Met, garnering an invitation to the season-ending All-High vs. All-Prep charity game. He scored a game-high eighteen points in a 77-54 victory.

Wootten arrived before the 1956-57 school year. That's when DeMatha and Cage really started to make their mark. For just the second time in fourteen games since DeMatha opened in 1946, the Stags beat Gonzaga. Cage had twenty-eight points and sixteen rebounds in the 62-59 victory.

The next morning, a story about the game in The Post started: "Unsung DeMatha High upset Gonzaga."

Cage would go on to score a Catholic league-record forty-one points in an 82-57 victory over Mackin, matching the school record he had set the previous year in a nonleague game against Charlotte Hall Military Academy. The Stags advanced to the Catholic league championship game that year, losing to Gonzaga, 84-61. Cage scored eighteen points but did not make a field goal in the second half. He averaged 22.6 points per game.

"His single most unique attribute, other than being very competitive, was just being a tremendous shooter," Spotts said. "He wasn't that tall and skinny as a rail – he looked like a walking two-iron. People don't realize he was a hell of a baseball pitcher.

"He was pretty frail-looking, kind of unassuming. But when he came down, he could fill it up. Back then, he had to rebound, too. Guys over six feet tall weren't tripping over each other -- there weren't that many."

Cage also had a nifty way to add to his point total and help his team.

"So many times guys would get fouled and Ernie ended up on the foul line," Spotts said. "They would blow the whistle and he would walk to the line. But I never heard anyone say, 'Hey, you weren't the guy who got fouled!' "

Indeed, Cage liked to have the ball in his hands. When the Stags played St. John's in a best-of-three series for the league's baseball title, nobody else took the mound for DeMatha. Cage pitched three complete games in eight days, including an eleven-inning, 3-2 loss in the second game. Cage followed that by throwing a six-hit shutout in the rubber match, a 6-0 DeMatha victory. It was the school's first league title in any sport.

"He was a great pitcher in baseball. It had something to do with accuracy -- he never walked anybody," said Wootten, who was an assistant coach on the baseball team. "If the three-point shot had been around in his day, he'd have records that would still stand. He was automatic from anywhere.

"The greatest thing about him as a shooter was he had the quickest release of anybody I ever saw. Magnificent touch, obviously. Anytime it didn't go in, it was almost like, 'That was an accident.' His shooting percentage was phenomenal."

Given how talented he was at seemingly anything he did in athletics, it was little surprise that dozens of college coaches pursued Cage.

Problem was, as Cage later told the Washington Evening Star, he was not terribly interested in schoolwork. That, in turn, limited his college choices.

"I wasn't dumb or anything, but I just never hit the books," Cage told the Evening Star. "I was a superb shooter – I can still put the ball in the hole if I'm standing still – but I couldn't get into too many schools because of my grades. "I wanted to go to North Carolina, and they were after me. In fact, there was a story in the paper saying I signed there. But I couldn't. My scores were too bad."

He wound up going to Mount St. Mary's College in Emmitsburg, Maryland. He averaged twenty points per game his freshman year and was not shy about shooting. Jim Phelan, the legendary Mount St. Mary's coach who went on to earn induction to the Naismith Memorial Hall of Fame, remembered one game at St. Francis University in Loretto, Pennsylvania. Cage passed up the team's point guard for an open layup, choosing instead to swish a twenty-five-footer. That gave Cage thirty-eight points, one off the gymnasium record.

"But here's our point guard stewing, [Cage] never got another shot in the last five minutes of the game," Phelan said. "They used to shoot one hundred foul shots in machine-gun fashion and he'd make ninety-six or ninety-seven of them. He was a great shooter."

Cage shot 88.4 percent from the foul line that season, which still stands as the second-highest percentage in school history.

The one thing that could stop Cage – the same thing that pushed him to Mount St. Mary's in the first place – again resurfaced. He did so poorly in school that he would not have been eligible to play basketball as a sophomore. So he transferred to Southeastern University in the District.

"A student he was not," Spotts said. "He was a sports junkie."

Cage never graduated from Southeastern. Instead, he did what most of the other males in his family did: He became a D.C. policeman, spending most of his career on the traffic beat. He also became a referee.

Talk about a tough combination of jobs. The next time anyone says (and means) "Nice job" to a traffic cop or a referee might be the first.

Cage enjoyed refereeing just as much as he did playing. He found the two positions required the same skill set.

"Being a policeman and being an umpire are similar because you have to be restrained," he told The Post's Neil Greenberger in 1984. "On the beat, you can't go around hitting people with a nightstick even though they are standing right up in your face calling you every name they can think of. It's the same when I'm umpiring – I can't go throwing people out of a game just for arguing. But luckily, I don't have to take as much from somebody in a softball game as I do in the street."

Cage did it all. Youth leagues. Junior high. Jayvee. Varsity. Small colleges and big-time freshman games. Anytime, anywhere, he would be there with his black-and-white zebra shirt and a whistle. There even was the wintry day in February 1972, when he was at home in New Carrollton, Maryland, settling in to watch the Clemson Tigers play the Maryland Terrapins at Cole Field House in College Park. Problem was, Lou Moser's refereeing partner could not make it because of the snowy weather. Cage got the call and sprang into action, hustling onto the court midway through the first half to work an Atlantic Coast Conference varsity game for the first time.

Not that his work impressed everyone.

"It doesn't make any difference to me who referees in this league," Clemson Coach Tates Locke told The Post's Paul Attner afterward. "All officials are bad; some are just worse than others."

Yep, being a referee or umpire gets you lots of adulation.

Cage was not limited to basketball. He umpired baseball games and officiated football games. He worked thirty-six years as a traffic cop before retiring and officiated countless games. When holding the game ball at an assembly at DeMatha to honor Wootten for his 900th career victory, Cage started sweating. He told folks he had never held onto the ball for so long, as a shooter or a referee.

"You could tell he loved the game," said the University of Maryland former coach Gary Williams, who as a budding young coach at American University got to know Cage. "I think he missed playing. Back then, it wasn't TV replays and all that. Yeah, there was a rulebook, but they called the game the way they thought it should be played. He liked aggressive, tough kind of players. I'm sure that's how he was. That's how we played at American, so we were always glad to see him."

Maybe some people CAN say nice things about referees – after the fact.

It was after he worked the Cotton Bowl football game in 1997 that Cage learned he had a brain tumor. He died on December 19, 1997, at age fifty-eight. His three marriages produced three children, including Candy Cage, the athletic director at Elizabeth Seton High School in Bladensburg, Maryland.

"I kind of regret not graduating," Ernie Cage told The Post's Steve Berkowitz in 1987. "I would have liked to be a high school coach or something like that, but like I said, sports and the police department was all I ever knew."

18. Sherman Douglas

It's not as if Sherman Douglas dominated the spotlight.

Name another basketball player to be named his local Player of the Year, then lose out on national Player of the Year honors to a peer from his same city.

Then this player went to a college that did not recruit him until the spring of his senior year – and, even then, was interested only because a more highly-touted prospect was not going to cut it academically.

Ego never was an issue for Sherman Douglas. A point guard's job is to run the offense and get the ball to teammates in scoring position -- though Douglas could score, too.

Finally getting his act together after a shaky start at Spingarn High in Northeast Washington, Douglas is now considered one of the finest point guards in Washington-area history.

He led Spingarn High to an undefeated season and the 1985 City Title.

He led Syracuse University to the NCAA tournament final as a sophomore in 1987 and completed his college career as the school's all-time leading scorer and the Big East Conference's all-time assist leader. In each of his final three seasons at Syracuse, Douglas was named all-Big East.

Then Douglas played eleven seasons in the NBA, cementing his nickname as "the General," with career averages of eleven points and 5.9 assists per game.

"Nothing was ever given," Douglas said. "It's like that when you don't go to a lot of camps. That hurts you with your publicity. Look at Boo Harvey – he went to a lot of camps, he was highly recruited."

It was only when Harvey, who had committed to play for Syracuse, was unable to meet the NCAA's minimum academic standards for eligibility, did the Orangemen look to Douglas.

"Some guys mature later," Douglas said. "In eleventh or twelfth grade, some guys get better. There wasn't any Internet back then. I wasn't highly recruited until Boo Harvey flunked out. Then here I go.

"I knew that I could play. I always had in my mind that I had the confidence. It's just getting people on board. I never doubted myself."

Perhaps the biggest challenge for Douglas growing up was not on the basketball court but in the classroom.

The youngest of five children born to Lorraine and Herbert Douglas, Sherman took an interest in basketball because – like most areas of the District – it was the game of choice in the Southeast neighborhood of Potomac Gardens. There was one court among the apartments. Win and stay on. Lose and – again, like most areas – you might have a long wait before you got back on.

"I was off a lot," Douglas said. "You were young and a lot of older guys didn't want to play with a younger kid."

Undeterred as an elementary schooler, Douglas would try to get on the court before the afternoon series of games began. That is when the younger players could shoot as much as they wanted, before the games started and they were relegated to watching.

At Hine Junior High, Douglas still did not earn much run. He played on the school team as an eighth-grader, then was cut the next year.

"I was just a knucklehead; my grades were not good," Douglas said. "The coach did a good job having me not on the team. He wanted me to keep my head on straight. … I was just immature. I wasn't focused. School, I didn't take it like I should have."

At that point, playing on the school team was not enough to motivate Douglas to do his schoolwork.

It took a little while for that idea to sink in.

After enrolling at Spingarn High – as opposed to the closer Eastern High, where his friends and siblings went to school – Douglas was academically ineligible to play as a sophomore. Instead of suiting up for the Green Wave, Douglas went back to the No. 9 Metropolitan Police Boys and Girls Club and played for its team, growing close to his coach and winning a league title.

"The coach threatened me that I didn't need to be back playing at Number Nine again that I needed to be playing high school basketball," Douglas said. "He used to pick me up and take me to practice and we had a nice little relationship. After he threatened me, I realized I did have talent. That woke me up."

Douglas had watched a few Spingarn games the previous season. The Green Wave had the makings of a strong team, led by center Michael Graham, who would go to Georgetown University and help the Hoyas win the 1984 national championship. Having received a pep talk that altered his outlook, Douglas wanted to join the team; he would repeat his sophomore year at Spingarn.

"I knew I didn't want to go to Eastern and I knew I didn't want to go to Anacostia. I wanted to give Spingarn another try," he said. "The lesson I learned is if I didn't have the grades, I wasn't going to play. I knew I had to pass some courses for that first semester if I wanted to be able to play for tryouts."

Douglas made the junior varsity in tryouts, but shortly was moved up to the varsity. Midway through the season, he became a starter. Somehow, the five-eight point guard had to reconcile playing with older, more- experienced teammates that only a year ago he had watched from the bleachers.

"I can remember watching them the first tenth-grade year and thinking, 'Could I do this? Was I big enough to play?'" Douglas said. "You see guys going from junior high to high school and the guys are taller as well as more muscular. They're bigger than you. You're thinking whether you can do it. It's different than playing against guys the same age. You're getting to play against guys who are six-eleven, six-seven, six-five. Those guys seemed big to me.

"Once I started, it felt good, but I still was the tenth-grader. You don't know your role yet. Most guys are in the twelfth grade and they're better than you. I was just distributing as a point guard. It's hard to take control of the team and you're a tenth-grader and they're seniors."

Not that Douglas struggled. In the Interhigh tournament championship game at the D.C. Armory, he made a go-ahead free throw with ten seconds left. With his teammates back on defense, Douglas missed his second attempt, but grabbed the rebound and Spingarn held on for a 57-55 victory over Anacostia.

"I was nervous back then," Douglas said. "Tenth grade? Think about this: You're playing for the first time in these big venues."

With Graham at Georgetown and Clarence Green at Cheyney State University, Spingarn was not as dominant during Douglas's junior season in 1983-84.

"We went from a Michael Graham-tall team to a small team," Douglas said. "From having a guy like Michael Graham in the middle – a straight-up animal! – to having young guys who didn't play varsity before. We had to go from a physical team to a track, finesse team. We were running, pressing, doing different things. I went from being a point guard to being a point guard shooting."

There were some highlights, though, as Douglas earned third-team All-Met honors. The most memorable came in late February, when Spingarn knocked off top-ranked Dunbar, which entered 21-0. Douglas made a 20-footer from the right side with five seconds left to tie it at 52-52 and force overtime.

In the second extra period, with eventual two-time All-Met Darryl Prue – Douglas's good friend – having fouled out, a steal led to a Douglas breakaway. Inexplicably, instead of going in for a layup, while being chased by two defenders Douglas did a three hundred sixty-degree spin while in the air and banked in a shot while being fouled, giving him twenty-three points in the 67-61 victory.

"I don't know what the hell I was thinking - I can't remember," Douglas said. "I remember Dunbar being packed. Sometimes, when you do a move, you don't know what the hell you've done and the coach is like, 'Oh, you made it.' "

"Put a big guy on him, he goes by them; put a small guy on him, he'll post up. He will figure out a way to get it done," said Prue, who later played with Douglas in a thirty-five-and-over league in Largo, Maryland.

"I always had a special admiration for him. He wasn't the flashiest guy, wasn't the fastest guy, didn't jump the highest. But he always did well. I thought he was underrated coming out of high school. We didn't go to a lot of camps back then."

Douglas was maturing on the court. He averaged 20.7 points per game that year. Spingarn went 24-6 and finished the season ranked tenth in the area by The Washington Post.

Yet Douglas was receiving scant interest from college recruiters.

"I can see it right now, myself, people who say girls mature faster than boys. I was the classic case," Douglas said. "I was taking class more focused -- knowing that if I didn't get my grades, I wasn't going to play. It was starting to mean more to me."

Douglas slowly was envisioning himself playing in college, potentially at a high level. He had grown up a fan of the Atlantic Coast Conference.

"How can I not like the Jefferson-Pilot game of the week? That is what I used to watch," he said. "It took until my high school years to become a Big East fan. Billy Packer and all that? I was there for that."

With an experienced lineup, Spingarn was ready for the 1984-85 season.

Ranked second in The Post to start the season behind – who else? – DeMatha, Douglas started the season with forty-eight points in a victory at DuVal. (The Spingarn football had scored a total of forty-one points in ten games that fall.) Then he scored thirty-six against Oxon Hill. Douglas and Robert Smith had nineteen points each in a late-January, 79-63 victory over fifth-ranked Coolidge. The Green Wave was 15-0 and counting, the accolades were coming.

From a February 21, 1985, story in The Post:

In the 1950s, the star was a player named Elgin Baylor. In the '60s, there was a jump-shooting guard named Dave Bing. The next decade produced all-metropolitans Harry Nickens and Diego McCoy. In 1980, Earl Jones migrated from West Virginia to lead Spingarn High School to the city championship. In the 32 years since Spingarn opened its doors in Northeast Washington, the school has turned out as many or more successful teams and players as any other school in the District of Columbia. But in all those years, with all those players, no Spingarn team of the past could have matched this year's squad for sheer entertainment value and, perhaps, success.

In the season's closing weeks, Douglas scored thirty-five points, passed to Robert Smith for a game-tying basket at the regulation buzzer and Spingarn held off Dunbar, 66-61 in double overtime to improve to 26-0 and clinch the Interhigh title.

Coach John Wood, though, did not want his players getting a big head as they sat atop The Post's rankings and eventually improved to 30-0 to set up a City Title showdown with second-ranked DeMatha at Cole Field House. DeMatha (29-1) was led by the twin towers of Danny Ferry and Jerrod Mustaf.

"You might be 30-0, but with Earl Jones and everybody else, I had teams that were better you," Wood told his players after practice one evening.

Wood also told the players that if the game was close, it was unlikely to go their way.

"It can't be close, because if it's close we're going to lose," Wood repeatedly said during preparations for the game. "We have to have a nice margin going to the fourth quarter."

He was not talking about the Green Wave choking in tight situations.

Before 12,115 fans, Douglas scored a game-high fourteen points with seven assists, leading the Green Wave to a 54-46 victory.

"They scouted us, they knew what we liked to do," Douglas said. "It was a defensive battle. We wanted to run. They probably wanted to slow it down a little bit."

Afterward, Smith approached University of Maryland basketball coach Lefty Driesell, watching courtside, to see if it was okay if the Spingarn players cut down the nets. There was one other interested college coach in attendance that night, Syracuse assistant Wayne Morgan, who had come to see Douglas play for the first time.

A few weeks earlier, Morgan had learned that prized recruit Harvey was unlikely to make the cut academically. The Orangemen still had star point guard Dwayne "Pearl" Washington and could make do without landing another player at the position. But if Morgan found someone he liked, Coach Jim Boeheim gave him the go-ahead to recruit the player.

Throughout the season, Morgan had been recruiting Coolidge center David Butler, a seven-footer who eventually went to a junior college and then helped Nevada-Las Vegas win the 1990 national title. Each time he went to Coolidge, Coach Frank Williams kept asking if Morgan had seen another player.

"Have you seen the General?" Williams would say.

"Who is that?" Morgan would reply.

"He's this little guy, who is unbelievable."

Finally, near the end of the season and without Harvey on the horizon, Morgan decided to take in a Spingarn game. One of the last people in the sold-out crowd to make it in the doors, Morgan sat near the top of the seating bowl in Cole Field House.

"I'm talking to people about Sherman and they keep saying he's this good little player, but he's five-nine, one hundred forty pounds and he's a two-guard," Morgan said. "It's a nip-and-tuck game, back and forth. At the end, DeMatha is losing, they start trying to press. And for the last five or six minutes of the game, Sherman brings the ball up, he handles the ball against pressure, not the other point guard. And he starts the offense, they throw it back to him and he scores. And he does that repeatedly."

Douglas's play had impressed Morgan. It also helped Douglas, not Ferry, earn All-Met Player of the Year honors. He averaged twenty-six points, six assists and five rebounds and scored more than thirty points nine times:

Talented, quick guard who can dominate a game ... shoots very well inside and outside and averaged 26 points per game for city champion Spingarn (31-0), the No. 1 team in the area ... averaged seven assists and three steals.

While others wondered whether Ferry – soon to be named USA Today's national Player of the Year -- would pick Duke or North Carolina, Douglas did not yet have any scholarship offers.

Syracuse soon changed that. After watching Douglas in the City Title Game, Morgan returned to campus and gave Boeheim a report.

"I think he's better than Boo," Morgan said.

"That's impossible," Boeheim replied. "Boo is an all-American."

But when Morgan brought his boss to a Capital Classic practice, Boeheim soon was convinced. After Douglas scored a team-high twenty-four points in a Capital Classic loss, the Orangemen offered a scholarship.

How late in the recruiting cycle was in when Douglas visited Upstate New York? He could see grass, not snow, on the ground.

"Think about that -- they came to me for grades," Douglas said. "They were not great [grades], but I could get into college.

"I liked it. I knew about Syracuse from seeing them on television, battling Georgetown and all that."

Once he arrived in Syracuse, though, Douglas was in for a shock.

"You know it's going to be cold, but you don't really know how cold," he said. "You're getting snow in October, and we're not talking an inch or two. They're talking lake-effect snow and we're talking feet. As well as going from a predominantly black school to a white, Jewish school. And I'm away from home. And I'm playing against legends. That scared me my freshman year."

As in high school, it took time for Douglas, now a six-footer, to get comfortable. At Syracuse, he got a boost from playing in practice against Washington, who often dialed it up a notch in games.

"By him not being a great practice player, he helped me out because I played hard and I did well, and it gave me some confidence and the coaches were like, 'Okay, he can play a little bit,'" Douglas said.

Douglas did not repeat his academic misadventures, though.

"I knew how to do enough to get by. I wasn't splitting the atom, I can tell you that much," Douglas said. "I could have my grades and get eligible. I knew I wanted to play and I knew I wanted to play big-time basketball. Syracuse was right there. It was at the top."

By that point, Douglas also was a pretty tough customer.

"One thing about being in D.C. -- people are going to talk trash, you've got to get used to it, you've got to focus on the game," he said. "You always want to state your case and tell people how good you are. Growing up where I did, it was a tough neighborhood. I wasn't about to take no s--- from nobody.

"Either you're going to have something nice or somebody is going to take it from you. You've got to stand up or you're going to be the guy with the 'Kick Me' sign on your back your entire life. People take advantage of the weak. You're either going to stand up or you're not. I didn't want to be one of the guys who was picked on or beat up. It wasn't going to be me."

As expected, Washington left the next spring for the NBA. Not that Syracuse's coaching staff was ready to hand a starting job to Douglas, as it continued to recruit point guards. Only when another recruit did not gain academic eligibility was Douglas certain to play.

"I was pretty much the only point guard there; I knew I was going to get some playing time," he said. "It was up to me to prove I could play. People put a lot of stock in high school all-Americans. I wasn't a Parade all-American first-team and all that. I knew I had to play really well if I wanted to keep my spot."

That he did. As a sophomore during the 1986-87 season, Douglas led the Orangemen to first place in the Big East regular season. He scored a Big East tournament-record thirty-five points in a semifinal victory over Pittsburgh. Syracuse reached the NCAA tournament championship game, losing to Indiana, 74-73, on Keith Smart's baseline jumper in the closing seconds.

"He came into Syracuse as a bright kid, but academically did not have a full toolbox," Morgan said. "He worked very hard. As a freshman, he was a guy that came in and was afraid to speak to anybody because he was self-conscious. As a senior, he was giving speeches to crowds of people.

"Everything Sherman has, he earned. He worked very hard to be where he is."

Douglas was named all-conference three times before being selected early in the second round of the 1989 NBA draft by the Miami Heat. He was a solid pro, his first two seasons being among his best. He averaged 14.3 and 7.6 assists as a rookie, and a career-high 18.5 points and 8.5 assists in his second season with the Heat. He went on to play for the Boston Celtics, Milwaukee Bucks, New Jersey Nets and Los Angeles Clippers before retiring after the 2001 season.

Douglas's oldest daughter, Demi, was an all-region high school basketball player in Georgia. He married his wife, Kyndall, in 2000 and they have two children: Kenyan and Demetri.

17. Louis Bullock

He was partly, if not directly, responsible for the emergence of two tiny private schools on the Washington-area basketball landscape. He still holds the record for the most points in the Capital Classic all-star game. In college, he was a sensational shooter but was also part of one of the NCAA's biggest scandals ever. As a pro, he played thirteen seasons in Europe.

Through it all, Louis Bullock has taken copious notes and has thought through some remarkable situations.

Someday soon, when he finally hangs up his high tops, he is going to have some good stories to tell.

"I've been chronicling everything because when I'm done playing, I'm planning to write a book," Bullock said before retiring. "I planned on doing it sooner."

Maybe he did not anticipate such a long career. But Bullock has a special talent: He can really shoot.

That is what helped him become a two-time All-Met in the mid-1990s, first as a junior at the Canterbury School in Accokeek, Maryland; then as a senior at Laurel Baptist Academy.

It is what made him such a desired college prospect, earning a scholarship to the University of Michigan, where he set numerous school records and still has made more three-point shots than all but one other player in Big Ten Conference history.

Bullock's name, though, can be found in few record books. Canterbury has closed. Laurel Baptist no longer exists, either. As for college, after it was discovered that a Michigan booster had paid thousands of dollars to four players, including Bullock, the school's penalties included vacating the games and records from those players' tenure.

When Bullock did not make an NBA roster after being a second-round pick of the Minnesota Timberwolves in 1999, he headed to Europe. Among his career highlights were leading the Italian league in scoring and earning league finals most valuable player honors as he led Real Madrid to the Spanish league title in 2005.

"I wasn't driven by the NBA. I always knew I was good enough to play because of how I played against guys that made it or were talked about," Bullock said. "I never went chasing after it. Like my dad, at the end of the day, you do what you have to do to take care of your family. Being a second-round pick and getting cut and not knowing what you are going to do next is a feeling I never want to go through again."

In Europe, Bullock learned, there was always a place for a shooter -- much like there was in the United States.

He grew up in Temple Hills, Maryland, and liked to create a ball of aluminum foil and shoot it into whatever "basket" he could find. Louis Bullock Sr. surprised his son by erecting a basketball hoop in the driveway for the youngster's seventh birthday and that made him "the popular kid on the block."

Problem was, the driveway was wide enough for only one car. Longer shots and room to pass the ball required running on the father's prized green grass, which soon was trampled.

"My dad loved his grass, but he sacrificed it for us to play basketball," Bullock said. "He would always tell me, 'Only two kids at a time,' trying to save his grass. But I wasn't the oldest guy playing and I couldn't tell them no. We would turn the grass into dirt, and he would take [the basket] down for a month at a time until he finally gave in and said okay."

Young Louis would be outside as much as possible, usually shooting on his new backboard, with the rim lowered to about nine feet to make shooting easier.

His love for basketball apparent, two older cousins came by the house on Bullock's eighth birthday and signed him up for basketball at the Silver Hill Boys and Girls Club. In fourth grade, he started playing on the team at Holy Family Catholic School. And he always kept shooting on that basket outside his house – which Bullock credits with honing his shooting stroke.

"I had a power line that ran across our driveway, [so] if you wanted to shoot from three-point range or anything around the top of the key, from the free throw line back, you had to shoot it over this wire or it would be a line drive," he said. "That's how I developed getting an arc on my shot. I had to shoot over that wire.

"Also, whenever my dad would come home from work, I would be playing outside. He would be tired, he couldn't stop and play, but he would always check me out and say, 'You have to get the ball over the front of the rim.'"

Louis Sr. worked days as a grocery store meat cutter and nights at the Government Printing Office, and he wanted his son to go to the nearby Gonzaga College High School. Bullock hit a growth spurt, gaining four inches in the summer before eighth grade. Suddenly, he was a hot prospect for high school coaches.

"That's when things kind of changed for me," Bullock said. "I was good, but a lot of my friends had been taller and more physically mature than I was. That was the moment I started to catch up with everybody."

Taft Hickman, the coach from Potomac High in nearby Oxon Hill, visited the Bullock house, hoping that young Louis would attend the neighborhood public school. Hickman, though, knew Bullock likely was bound for private school.

"Some of my friends had also decided to go to [Bishop] McNamara, and we were trying to convince my dad to let me go so we could play jayvee together," Bullock said. "I didn't know anybody at Gonzaga, and McNamara had a better team. And they offered me a scholarship, so that helped convince him as well."

At McNamara, Bullock was the star of the junior varsity team but it was hardly a smooth year. He had been a good student, but now his report cards were littered with C's. Popularity interfered with schoolwork, and his father threatened to send him to Gonzaga if things did not improve.

Naturally, with Louis headed for the varsity as a sophomore, his report card got a bit worse. Instead of going to Gonzaga, though, his parents sent him to a school he had never heard of, that seemed to be located in the middle of nowhere, with a Rebel mascot anointed by its coach and without a gym, with forty students in seventh through twelfth grades.

Canterbury hardly seemed like somewhere Louis Bullock wanted to be.

"I had no choice," said Bullock, who wound up repeating a year of school at Canterbury because he had done so poorly academically at McNamara. "I ended up going there.

"When I left McNamara, it was like, 'He fell off the face of the map,' because nobody knew where Canterbury was. ... You couldn't even see the school from the street. You could only see the church. You get off Indian Head Highway and take a windy road with a house here or there.

"Myself, you can't imagine who would build a house out there. You come up on the church and behind the church was living quarters for nuns and they turned it into a school. All the classrooms were bedroom-sized!"

The one thing Canterbury did have was a young, energetic coach, who was still in college himself, and an assistant coach who Bullock knew from the boys club.

"I was just looking to coach, be an assistant coach while I was in college," said Chris Chaney, who started for two years on the varsity at Southern High in Anne Arundel County before graduating in 1989. "I started looking at private schools and that was one of them. They said they weren't looking for an assistant coach; they were looking for a head coach."

Chaney was hired. He had Frank Pfeiffer as an assistant. That first season, before Bullock arrived, the team occasionally practiced outdoors. During Bullock's first year at Canterbury in 1991-92, G. Gardner Shugart Middle School in Temple Hills was Chaney's gymnasium of choice. All of the team's games had to be played on the road. The roster became loaded with players in search of better opportunities to showcase their skills or to get a fresh start.

It did not take long for Canterbury to become a powerhouse. Chaney left after that first season, but Pfeiffer took over and nothing changed. The coaches tried to schedule the best opponents they could find, caring little about winning and more about establishing their program.

"I knew he was going to be special, but I was young myself and just figuring out what I wanted to do more than be worried about how special he was," Chaney said. "The first game he ever played for me, I think he had forty-four points against Spalding. Spalding wasn't very good back then, but forty-four was forty-four."

Early in the 1992-93 season, Bullock scored twenty-two points as Canterbury beat Archbishop Carroll, 71-65, in the semifinals of the first Beltway Classic at Dunbar High. He went on to earn fourth-team All-Met honors, the only sophomore on any of the four teams named by The Washington Post.

As a junior in 1993-94, Bullock began posting unbelievable numbers. Against Colonial Beach, he had fifty-three points and seventeen rebounds in a 114-76 victory. He scored twenty-nine points in an 80-77 victory over McKinley Tech, which was led by eventual Georgetown standout Victor Page. Canterbury finished the season 29-3 with a fifteen-game winning streak. Bullock averaged twenty-seven points, nine rebounds and three assists and was named first-team All-Met, having scored in double figures in all but one of his ninety-four games at Canterbury.

Then things got a bit goofier.

A few weeks before the 1994-95 school year started, Canterbury's administration decided to downgrade its basketball program and scale back to a schedule more befitting a school its size.

Pfeiffer tried to get most of the team to transfer to National Christian Academy in Fort Washington, Maryland. Chaney, though, had just been hired to start a team at Laurel Baptist in Laurel, Maryland.

"We had gotten so much attention. I know Frank wanted to take the school to the level that Stu Vetter was doing [at St. John's/Prospect Hall by this point], but financially they couldn't do it," Bullock said. "More and more guys wanted to transfer and come. By my junior year, there were guys all around the D.C. area trying to get into Canterbury. They couldn't pay the tuition in a lot of situations.

"Canterbury took the stance they couldn't offer any more scholarships. It became a standoff and I had stayed close with Chris Chaney. … I decided to go there for my senior year."

And what was Laurel Baptist like?

"It was ever smaller," Bullock said, noting that there were forty-seven students in kindergarten through high school. "And eleven of us were on the basketball team. The school was actually across the street from Pallotti High School in the old Laurel Boys and Girls Club building, on the top floor.

"There were three classrooms. The high school, all grades, were in one class. The middle school had their class and the elementary school had their class. You had your work station and you did your work. The teacher would come around and check your work and if it was right, you could progress to the next level or exercise they had. It was a crazy setup. But I was already qualified, had passed my SATs."

As he tried to narrow his college choices, Bullock had it down to Maryland and Michigan. He wanted to play for the hometown school. After taking an official visit to Ann Arbor, Michigan, he went over to Cole Field House to meet with Maryland Coach Gary Williams, taking his cousin, Nathaniel, one of the cousins who started him at Silver Hill. Nathaniel Bullock posed the question to Williams: What kind of playing time would Louis be looking at as a freshman, and would he have a chance to start?

"I knew I wanted to play, but I didn't have the courage to ask that. I wasn't going to ask and I didn't ask my cousin to ask," Bullock said.

Williams, as usual, was blunt in his response.

"I've got a senior backcourt. I've got Duane Simpkins and Johnny Rhodes, and I'm very loyal to my seniors," Williams said. "So Louis might not play that much. But from his sophomore year on, it's going to be his team."

"I couldn't imagine not playing," Bullock said, noting that Michigan had had its Fab Five freshman class in 1991-92. "Steve Fisher at Michigan told me he didn't have a determined starting lineup. He said, 'I've started five freshmen. You can come in, compete, and if you win the job you can play.'

"So I decided to go away from home."

Before leaving, though, Bullock enjoyed his senior season. He averaged 25.7 points, 8.7 rebounds, 8.4 assists and three steals. The Eagles went 36-5 and finished the season ranked third in the Washington area. They beat Vetter's Prospect Hall team as Bullock made all of his eleven free throws in overtime and finished with forty points in a 62-56 victory. Junior Nate James, who eventually went to Duke University, scored twenty-one points for the losing squad, which had been undefeated and ranked fourth nationally by USA Today.

At season's end, Bullock was The Post's All-Met Player of the Year and earned an invitation to the McDonald's All-American Game, where he won the three-point shootout. He also scored forty points in the Capital Classic as the Capital All-Stars lost to the U.S. All-Stars, 124-121, in overtime.

At Michigan, Bullock earned a starting position early on, made a school single-season record one hundred one three-point shots as a freshman and never let up. He finished his career with 2,224 points, which would rank third among all players ever at the school. He made 86.9 percent of his free throws, and his five hundred five foul shots would be the most ever by a Wolverine. He made more three-pointers than any player in Big Ten Conference history.

But Bullock's name is nowhere to be found in the Michigan record books. After an unwieldy investigation that began after four Wolverines and recruit Mateen Cleaves got into a late-night car accident in February 1996, it was determined that booster Ed Martin had given Bullock, Chris Webber, Maurice Taylor and Robert Traylor six hundred sixteen thousand dollars in loans that they could repay after they turned professional. The NCAA, FBI, IRS and Justice Department all were involved in the investigation.

"That was a part of my life that really shaped and just helped me become who I am today. It was such an up-and-down experience," Bullock said. "You had the highs of playing in a big-time program, but not really realizing what it's like, the other things that go along with it.

"It was all that I could hope for basketball-wise. Definitely, I wasn't prepared for being in a big program like that. You can't imagine being eighteen, nineteen years old and being interrogated the whole time. It was a crazy experience but definitely helps you grow and makes me think if I had a chance to do it all over again, would I have chosen to do things differently? But I still would have chosen to go to Michigan.

"I won't say I was sheltered, but there is a big difference [from a small private school to a large state university]. I was always in such structured situations where, once you don't have someone telling you that you have to do this or that, you become amazed at the leniency around you and the things you can get away with.

"I didn't realize it at the time, that college is such a big business. It's wins and losses for the coaches. They have to get W's to keep their jobs. How far will you go to get that next top recruit or Mickey D's All-American?"

When Michigan was appealing to the NCAA for leniency, administrators asked Bullock to write a letter detailing what he had been through. That letter, though, never made it to the sanctioning body's headquarters in Kansas City, Missouri.

"I wrote it according to how things really happened," Bullock said. "Instead of writing it and saying, 'It's all my fault,' I said, 'This is what happened.' [A Michigan official] called me back and said, 'Hey, can you be a thousand times more apologetic?'"

Bullock was not interested in any editing.

"That was an insult to me, because it was apparent what was going on there," Bullock said. "It was obvious. One of those things, 'Don't ask, don't tell. You know what's going on, but hey, prove it.'"

The letter never was sent.

After completing his eligibility at Michigan, Bullock was selected by Minnesota in the second round of the 1999 NBA draft. The Timberwolves immediately traded his rights to the Orlando Magic. Bullock was cut during training camp and headed to Europe, where he played his entire professional career. He is fluent in Italian and Spanish.

Bullock and his wife, Maya, have two daughters, Layla and Shaena.

16. James Brown

If the All-American player had chosen to go to a college that took its basketball seriously – instead of Harvard University -- maybe he would have had a lengthy and successful pro career.

Then again, maybe if he had gone down that road, he never would have gotten into sales, never would have learned the art of persuasion, never would have had the opportunity to get in front of a camera and, perhaps, never would have become the television star he is today.

Sure, there are fleeting thoughts of what might have been, but James Brown prefers not to play the "What if?' game.

"There are no guarantees, and who is to say I wouldn't be injured?" Brown said. "My mother and father, God bless them, drove that point home. Of course you think about it, but I don't dwell on it. Even though things didn't work out [with basketball] after Harvard, if I had to make the decision over again, I'd do it again."

Only rarely has such a basketball star headed to the Ivy League.

Brown still remembers that day he walked into Coach Morgan Wootten's office at DeMatha Catholic High School and saw the recruiting letter from Harvard on the desk. Brown had admired former Princeton star Bill Bradley – who initially planned to go to Duke University before changing his mind – and thought Harvard would present similar opportunities.

But with the likes of North Carolina Coach Dean Smith and dozens of others trying to woo Brown in the late 1960s, his decision was not easy.

After each of his five official, college-paid campus visits, Brown told the coach he was ninety-nine percent certain he would attend that school.

Good thing that Wootten had a policy forbidding players from making verbal (although nonbinding) commitments while on college trips. Stags players were required to return to school in Hyattsville, Maryland, and discuss their options with their families and with Wootten before making any decisions. (Imagine trying to enforce that regulation in the Internet age!) When a player was on campus, Wootten thought, it was like a honeymoon. An easily influenced teenager was going to all the best restaurants and fanciest places in town and was no match for the honed sales pitches of college coaches on their home court.

"I live faithfully by this – I never told them who to marry and didn't tell them where to go to school," Wooten said. "I never pushed or encouraged. I would tell them where not to go, if I thought it was a bad spot for them. It was usually because of illegalities."

As a six-foot, five-inch guard thrust into playing center at DeMatha because the team needed him to fill that position, Brown saw his share of funny business.

"A number of these guys were being offered cars, money, clothes; a lot of inducements to go wherever," Brown said. "There was a major ACC school – not here, not Maryland, not North Carolina – that had offered me a scholarship to come there. And when I made the decision to go to Harvard, a very influential alum, a successful entrepreneur in the Washington area, came to the Morgan Wootten basketball camp and told me I might want to reconsider my decision to go to Harvard because he had helped my dad with some of his bills.

"But by then, I had been well schooled by Morgan Wootten, and I said, 'I'm sorry, but that's between you and my father.'"

More than forty years after the fact, Brown still will not identify the school, although he thinks the booster was acting on his own and was not under the direction of any coach or administrator.

"It just goes to show you that college sports is rife with those kind of inducements under the table," he said.

But the inducement that interested Brown the most was a trip to the U.S. Capitol, where Sen. Edward M. Kennedy of Massachusetts – Harvard, Class of 1956 – had invited him to visit.

"We got on the subway [from Kennedy's office] and went to the Capitol because he had to cast a couple votes, and he introduced us to some senators," Wootten said.

Then Ted Kennedy, who played end on the Crimson football team, set his sights on Brown.

"James, there is only one Harvard," he said, a pitch that later was echoed by then-Boston Celtics President Red Auerbach, a friend of Wootten's.

Kennedy did not discuss any other schools. He told of a trip he had recently taken to go mountain climbing in the Alps and tried to converse with locals with broken English. But when he mentioned Harvard, Wootten said in retelling the story, they understood him completely.

"So James started looking into Harvard and put Dean on hold," Wootten said. "Then he went up to Harvard and he got sold."

Unsure whether he could get into Harvard, Brown took up Crimson Coach Bob Harrison on an offer for early acceptance, provided Brown would take it.

The deal was done.

But a short time later, a letter from UCLA arrived in the mail. The Bruins were starting their run of their seven consecutive NCAA championships. Coach John Wooden already was a legend. Denny Crum was his energetic assistant. Brown knew he had shaken hands with the folks at Harvard, but this was one trip he desperately wanted to take.

"Mom, I have to visit there," he told Mary Ann Brown, the matriarch of a family in which James was the oldest of four boys and one girl.

Her response was succinct: "You gave your word and you have to follow it."

James Brown would go to Harvard.

It was a curious landing spot for a player with such a pedigree. James was no star as a youngster – he still remembers blowing the uncontested layup at an eighth-grade pep rally at Bertie Backus Junior High in Northeast Washington. He ended up at DeMatha only after Wootten came to see his CYO baseball teammate, Steve Garrett, play in a tournament and Brown talked his way into a chance to play basketball for Wootten.

But in high school, Brown exploded. He was on the jayvee as a freshman, then started on the varsity for three years. (Adrian Dantley, four years later, would become the first ninth-grader to start at DeMatha.)

Brown made All-Met as a junior and repeated that honor as a senior, adding All-American awards. But perhaps the game for which he is most remembered is a game for which he never even dressed.

It was March 1969, in the annual season-ending Knights of Columbus Tournament at Catholic University. Brown had passed out from exhaustion during the fourth quarter of the Stags' 78-65 semifinal victory over St. Agnes of Rockville Centre, New York, and was taken to a hospital. The next day, preparing to face a McKinley Tech team that had beaten them, 68-55, earlier in the season, DeMatha's players draped Brown's warmup jacket over a chair and left it unoccupied. It probably would have made a nice seat for Brown, who – unbeknownst to his parents, teammates and coaches -- slipped out of Providence Hospital and walked over to Catholic University to watch the game, a 95-69 DeMatha victory.

"When they found out I wasn't going to be there, a number of the McKinley guys went out and partied the night before," Brown said, noting that had he not gone to DeMatha, he would have been playing for McKinley.

Sitting in the bleachers near the end of the court, Brown did his best not to attract attention. Some fans realized who he was – *how could you miss him!* – but he tried to quiet the buzz before finally joining his teammates on the court after their victory.

"I didn't want to let Coach Wootten know I was there," Brown said, adding that "my parents weren't too pleased I had done that."

"That is always referred to as one of the great victories in DeMatha history," Wootten said.

The victory also set off a furor around Washington. The morning after the game, The Washington Post published its season-ending basketball rankings, with DeMatha first and McKinley second. It seemed logical, given the Stags' 26-point victory in the season's final game *without their star player*. But McKinley's team and supporters said that the Trainers never would have played in the tournament if they had known their Number One ranking was at stake, and that in previous years The Post had released its final rankings before the Knights of Columbus Tournament. McKinley offered to play a rubber match, an idea endorsed by The Post. And when DeMatha rejected that idea, The Post "cancelled" its final rankings and "reverted" back to the previous rankings. Naturally, DeMatha still asserts that it finished the 1968-69 season Number One in the area.

There is one other message hidden in the story of the Knights of Columbus Tournament: Brown never wanted to be in the spotlight. Sure, he enjoyed his success and the attention thrust his way. One of the all-time great recruiting tricks came shortly after the season, when the University of Maryland's newly hired basketball coach Lefty Driesell, ran a "Most Wanted"-style, quarter-page ad in The Post, with the headline "We Want You . . . at the University of Maryland." Underneath it were mug shots of Brown, Jim O'Brien of Stuart High, Floyd Lewis of Western High and Dave Freitag of St. John's. (All four made The Post's All-Met team in 1969.) Such a ploy would no doubt be frowned on by today's NCAA.

"It was [assistant coach] George Raveling's idea," Driesell said. "It was in every paper in the country: 'Is this what's going on in college?' I checked before we put it in there and had the lawyers read it. People said you shouldn't have done it. I said 'shouldn't have' isn't against the rules."

Four days later, though, Brown announced he would go to Harvard.

At Harvard, though he three times was named All-Ivy League, Brown said he could not maintain the work ethic that had driven him to succeed at DeMatha. Growing up, he would spend countless hours at St. Ann's Infant and Maternity Home, where the was an outdoor court and he often worked alone on his game, repeating the drills that Wootten and St. John's Coach Joe Gallagher taught at their summer camp:

Dribble with both hands. Right-handed hook shots. Left-handed hook shots. Tap drills.

Brown did those religiously.

At home, he did hours of toe raises on the steps – which he credits for the leaping ability that allowed him to dunk even when the basket was raised to more than eleven feet.

But at Harvard, he said, he enjoyed being the big man on campus. The Crimson players had talent but did not realize their potential. And when it came time to chase his dream of playing in the NBA, things caught up to Brown. Picked in the fourth round of the NBA draft by the Atlanta Hawks in 1973, Brown was the last player cut.

Auerbach invited him to the Celtics' training camp the next year; again, Brown was the final cut. Auerbach urged Brown to go to Europe, season his game against strong competition and take another shot at the NBA. Brown, though, was ready to move on.

"I gave it two good shots," Brown said recently. "At age fifty-nine, I can look back and I can say I understand why I didn't make it. Now, I don't want to let an opportunity go by where I don't make it because I didn't pay the price."

Brown worked in sales, first for Xerox and then for Eastman Kodak. At the same time, he found a second job working in television, first as the color analyst for twenty Washington Bullets road games each season. Then he found work as a fill-in anchor, including a not-so-proud moment during his first sportscast when a videotape did not roll and viewers could see an the top of Brown's head as he gave an animated description of the highlights they were supposed to be watching.

Years later, after working his way into full-time employment as a television sports anchor, Brown had similar travails during his first NFL game as the play-by-play man. Producers and directors, though, were willing to work with him and provide second chances.

Today, Brown is one of the nation's top sports broadcasters. He hosts "NFL Today" each Sunday on CBS. He is a co-founder and principal of Brown Technology Group and recently published his memoirs, "Role of a Lifetime: Reflections on Faith, Family and Significant Living." Brown has a daughter, Katrina, and he and his wife, Dorothy, reside in Bethesda, Maryland.

15. Jo Jo Hunter

It is eerie, even unsettling, to read about Anthony "Jo Jo" Hunter.

Go back to February 1976. Hunter was a senior at Mackin High School, tearing up the competition, leading the Washington area in scoring, earning first-team All-Met honors and thinking about following Moses Malone by going from the preps to the pros.

A few days after scoring thirty-eight points during an overtime loss to DeMatha, Hunter was the subject of a long feature story in The Washington Post.

This is what Trojans Coach Harry Rest said: "This is the first time in his life he has had everything going for him. When I see the Anthony Hunter of today, I think of a life saved."

Hunter, who lived with an assistant coach for his final 1½ years of high school, said: "I came up the hard way but I handled it. I can look back and see that I did a good job of containing myself. I made the jump away from the kind of life I got closer to than I wanted.

"If I make it in pro basketball some day, it will mean the same to me as what I've done so far, but not more. I'm sort of halfway there. But what I've done with myself already is as important as making the pros."

But after putting things together to finish his high school career, Hunter never could quite maximize what seemed to be unlimited potential.

After two seasons playing for the University of Maryland, Hunter transferred. He planned to enroll at the University of Nevada-Las Vegas, but that did not pan out and he wound up playing for the University of Colorado. He was a sixth-round draft pick of the Milwaukee Bucks but never played in the NBA. He had a brief career in the minor leagues and abroad.

For fifteen years, however, Hunter played with a different number on his jersey. In 1997, he was sentenced to between 14 and 43 years in federal prison after being found guilty in the robbery of two Washington-area jewelry stores. He was released on parole in July 2012.

"I want to get the message out that prison is not cool and it's not what they think it is," Hunter told the Boulder Daily Camera in 2007. "Even though this is a place of indignity and no integrity or compassion and it's about survival, there is a lot of talent in here. There's a lot of kids in here. It's a shame they have to come here to find out their talents. ... I just have to survive in here. I think my niche when I get out is to pass my experiences on to other kids. This is a revolving door that someone or somebody needs to address."

In 2011, Hunter told Dave McKenna of the *Washington City Paper*: "I've done my time as good as I could. I made mistakes and bad choices, but I've been able to help mold some guys in here. I think I deserve a second chance."

Now that he was released from prison, Jo Jo Hunter wants to be the one to set some young people in the right direction.

After all, few have possessed the talent that many thought made him a seemingly can't-miss superstar.

Growing up near McKinley High School in Northwest Washington, Hunter sparkled on the court from an early age. Rest, who was thirty-two years old when he became the head coach at Mackin in 1970, remembers the first time he saw Hunter: A junior high school basketball coach brought over two students – one in ninth grade and Hunter, who was in eighth grade – for Rest to look at.

"Keith [Herron] and Duck [Williams] happened to be in the gym, so I said to let them go ahead and work out," Rest said. "I told him that I would take the ninth-grader if he would send me the eighth-grader. The next year, I cut the ninth-grader, who was then a tenth-grader."

Cutting Hunter, though, was never an option. After a teammate was declared ineligible, Rest tried a few other players in the starting lineup before turning to Hunter. Then Hunter got a chance at point guard. Once in the starting five, Hunter never left. And by the middle of that season, everyone knew him by his nickname.

"He is an unbelievable fifteen-year-old," Rest told The Post at the time. "He stabilizes our offense. He has great composure. He looks just like Jo Jo White [of the Boston Celtics]. But I can't get Hunter to shoot enough. That's my problem."

Of course, Mackin had plenty of other capable shooters, led by Williams and the Herron twins, Keith and Larry. The Trojans finished the season ranked second in the area by The Post.

"Jo Jo was really quick and shifty," said former DeMatha guard Pete Strickland, who was two years ahead of Hunter. "What a great team that was. They had about nine Division I players. When they played DeMatha, I think there were eighteen Division I players on those rosters that day. Even as a young sophomore, I had a sense this basketball is as good as it was going to get."

Throughout his time at Mackin, Hunter just kept getting better. The Trojans spent part of the 1973-74 season atop The Post's rankings and he was second-team All-Met as a junior in the 1974-75 season.

By his senior year, everyone everywhere knew of Hunter. Howard Garfinkel, who ran the prestigious Five-Star summer basketball camps, called him "the best guard to come out of Washington." The Trojans were ranked fifth nationally before the season by Street and Smith's basketball magazine. Everything was lined up and Hunter did not disappoint, scoring twelve of his thirty-five points in the first quarter of a 109-66 victory over Anacostia. Then Mackin traveled to the Norfolk Invitational, where, playing on a sprained ankle, Hunter averaged thirty-two points per game to earn most valuable player honors and lead the Trojans to the championship.

"He wore one high top and one low top" to help his injured ankle, Rest said. "They told me that every kid in Norfolk wore one high top and one low top the next day!"

That was not the only way that other players tried to copy Hunter. He had an unusual, sweet shooting stroke, with one hand under the ball and the other on the side guiding the ball.

"Everybody imitated his jump shot – that jump in the air, had one hand on the ball and move the guide hand off," said Morgan State University basketball Coach Todd Bozeman, who grew up in Washington and was five years younger than Hunter. "That was hilarious. It was just the intensity with which he played and the way he attacked the game. He was relentless, the way he played. He'd go one hundred miles an hour and then he would stop and jump and sit in the air, and that jump shot would come off and be smooth as silk."

Hunter was scoring so much – with at least twenty points in fifteen of Mackin's first eighteen games – that he earned another nickname: "the Magician."

Hunter was relatively quiet off the court and – despite constant problems at home -- almost always was smiling. By his senior year, he spent most of his time at the home of Trojans assistant coach Ed Meyers. He had terrific power for a guard and was not scared of anything, whether it was driving into the paint against taller opponents or jumping center. He scored thirty-two points in a 77-71 victory over DeMatha and had thirty-three points, nine rebounds and six assists in a 70-59 victory over St. John's in the Metro Conference tournament final.

Hunter sprained an ankle during practice the day before his final regular season game, but that was not much of an impediment.

"I told him the game wasn't that meaningful, so stay home," Rest said. "I'm in the locker room, giving a great speech and how he carried us all year and we need to pick up for him. And right in the middle, Jo Jo shows up."

He showed up on the court, too, scoring fifty-seven points in a 104-58 victory over McNamara.

At season's end, Hunter had led the area is scoring, averaging twenty-eight points per game, and was a first-team All-Met. The Philadephia 76ers had been spotted scouting him, though Hunter soon would decide to go to college. Hunter and Carroll star Billy Bryant wanted to play together in college.

Hunter had considered most of the schools in the Atlantic Coast Conference as well as Rutgers, Indiana, Notre Dame, San Francisco, Nevada-Las Vegas, Kentucky and Louisville.

In the spring, Hunter traveled to South Bend, Indiana, to visit Notre Dame. A few nights later, he attended the Maryland Terrapins' season-ending team banquet. The guest speaker? Muhammad Ali.

A few days later, Hunter was signing scholarship papers to play for the Terps and Lefty Driesell. Bryant joined him. New assistant coach Wil Jones, just hired from Robinson Secondary School in Fairfax, had landed a pair of hotshot recruits.

"Lefty asked me, 'Can you recruit?' And I said, 'I'm from Washington -- I can recruit better than you!" Jones said. "I loved Lefty. He made basketball relevant in Washington, all that talk about making it the UCLA of the east. He said there were two great basketball players in Washington I could get, Jo Jo Hunter and Billy Bryant. I raised those boys like I raised these dogs. The athletic director at the time, Jim Kehoe, doubted me, but I told him to give me ten thousand dollars for every [All-American recruit] I get there!"

Once in College Park, though, things did not go according to script. The Terrapins struggled as an every-man-for-himself attitude prevailed.

Eventually, Driesell forced Hunter and Bryant to not live together, hoping to eliminate any cliques. It hardly worked. Even though he averaged 11.1 points per game as a sophomore, things were tumultuous for Hunter. In January, he missed curfew, skipped a team meeting and pregame meal, and was suspended for one game. In May, he announced he was transferring to Nevada-Las Vegas.

"I told him to get as far away [from home] as he could," Driesell said, believing that Hunter would benefit from a fresh start.

Life on the Strip, though, did not work out, either. Although he reportedly spent the summer working at the famed Flamingo hotel, by August Hunter had decided to enroll at Colorado.

It was in Boulder that he found a measure of stability. After sitting out one year to satisfy NCAA transfer requirements and become eligible at his new school, Hunter got off to a sizzling start. He made game-winning jumpers to knock off Oklahoma, the Big Eight Conference defending champion, and then Oklahoma State.

Hunter led Colorado in scoring in both of his seasons in Boulder, averaging 14.9 points per game as a junior and 19.1 as a senior. He made all sixteen free throws in a 78-68 victory over Iowa State in his first season playing for the Buffaloes, which is still tied for the school record for the most without a miss in one game. As a senior during the 1980-81 season, Hunter had a pair of thirty-point games and earned first-team all-Big Eight honors.

Despite playing just two seasons in a Buffaloes uniform, Hunter still ranks thirty-sixth on the school's career scoring charts.

Hunter did not graduate from Colorado, but that June he was selected by the Milwaukee Bucks in the sixth round of the NBA draft.

However, he did not make the Bucks' roster and bounced around a bit, spending one season in the Continental Basketball Association and then playing overseas. After returning to the Washington area in the mid-1980s, according to reports during his trial, he coached in local basketball leagues and worked as a paralegal, courier and personal trainer.

In July 1996, Hunter was arrested and charged with robbing two jewelry stores in Northwest Washington with an ex-girlfriend. The next April, a D.C. Superior Court jury found Hunter guilty of eleven felony charges in connection with stealing $350,000 of gems and watches and shooting a clerk in the arm during one heist. Much of his time was spent at the medium-security Federal Correctional Institution in Cumberland, Maryland.

14. Austin Carr

Perhaps no one was better at taking advantage of a situation more than Austin Carr.

Early in his freshman season at Mackin High, Carr was given the chance to move into the starting lineup because a teammate was sick. Carr played so well that he never came off the bench the rest of his high school career.

Defenders knew they had to put all their energy into guarding the sharpshooting Carr. But give him just a sliver of opportunity, a brief moment to break free, and Carr would knock down a shot for another two points.

There are few Washington-area players who scored two thousand points in high school.

Then, at the University of Notre Dame, the six-foot, four-inch guard took things a bit further. In three seasons – freshmen were ineligible to play intercollegiate athletics in the late 1960s – he scored 2,560 points. That was 34.6 points per game!

Even though more than four decades have passed and the NCAA now permits four years of athletic eligibility, the Notre Dame record book still reads like Carr's autobiography, because he still holds dozens of school records:

Most points in a career. Most points in a season (1,106). Most points in a game (sixty-one). Most points in a home game (fifty-five). Most points in a road game (fifty). Most points in a loss (fifty-four).

Most fifty-point games (nine). Most forty-point games (twelve). Most thirty-point games (twenty-three). Most consecutive twenty-point games (fifty-eight, or every game his junior and senior years).

The list goes on and on. His sixty-one-point performance against Ohio in 1970 remains the most points scored in an NCAA tournament game.

He was a scorer as a pro, too, averaging more than twenty points in each of his first three seasons with the Cleveland Cavaliers. He played ten years in the NBA, averaging 15.4 points per game.

Not too shabby for a guy who once thought he was going to be a .330-hitting catcher. Even after he figured out that basketball was the way to go, Carr excelled because he knew how to move without the ball and get open for just enough time to find his shot, regardless of how opponents tried to keep him off the scoreboard. Again, he was taking advantage of that small opportunity and making opponents pay.

"I guess it's instincts," said Carr, who now works as director of community relations for the Cavaliers and is the color analyst on the team's television broadcasts.

He said Mackin Coach Paul Furlong "taught me how to use angles, how to play the angles. Once I learned how to slow down, I used the angles because the defense didn't know where I was going -- only I knew where I was going. When I started, I would go too fast. I wouldn't use the picks. Again, you have to play on a team where people pass the ball to each other. We had a great team [at Mackin] because we shared the ball."

Carr's attitude and tireless work ethic can be traced to his formative years, growing up in the River Terrace area of Northeast Washington. The second of five boys born to Lula and Austin Sr., he played plenty of sports in his neighborhood and in CYO leagues for Our Lady Queen of Peace near the Fort Dupont Park in Southeast.

"When I was growing up, we were lucky to have a community that supported youth sports," Carr said. "I played a lot of baseball and football; basketball was a throw-in. We didn't play basketball in my community. I played that in CYO. That's how I got into basketball and started to play. When I went to ninth grade, they didn't have a football team at Mackin. I had to play baseball and basketball."

Beginning when Carr was in the third grade, his father sent all of the boys to Catholic schools, starting at Holy Redeemer on New Jersey Avenue in Northwest Carr was a fullback and linebacker on the football field and a catcher on the baseball diamond, where a frequent teammate was future NFL wide receiver Reggie Rucker.

On the basketball courts at local playgrounds, Carr eventually met Bill Butler and Richie Coleman and saw the success they enjoyed at Mackin. (Butler would be All-Met in 1963 and 1964, Coleman in 1965.) Carr wanted to play for the Trojans, too, and enrolled at Mackin for the 1963-64 school year.

Although private schools did recruit athletes in those days, Furlong was unaware of the talented player who had just started at the school.

"I'm walking down the hall after school one day and a kid comes up to me and says, 'Mister Furlong, you need to go to the gym and see someone in there,'" Furlong said. "It took me ten seconds to figure out who he was talking about. He had heard an announcement for all the freshmen to go to the gym after school for tryouts.

"That was the first time I laid eyes on him. I told him, 'You can hang around for a while.' Of course, he practiced for the varsity for the next four years."

Carr made the varsity as a freshman, beginning the season as a reserve. A few games in, though, with Mackin preparing for an eight-team holiday tournament up North Capitol Street at Archibishop Carroll, guard Lawrence Jones became sick. Carr would take his place in the starting five.

"I got fifteen or seventeen points in that first game and never looked back after that," Carr said.

Call him the Washington high school version of Lou Gehrig, if you will. Moving Carr into the starting lineup might have been one of the shrewdest moves Furlong ever made.

"I can't think of a more coachable player I ever had," Furlong said. "Everything you taught him, he immediately started working on it and doing what you told him. Every practice, he played hard. I changed his shooting motion. He used to shoot off his shoulder. I got him to shoot more out front, over his shooting eye, not to throw the ball so much but to use his wrist. And he would go in the gym and work on it at lunchtime."

Carr attributed his determination to his father. Austin Sr. had been a good athlete; he played tennis and baseball and boxed. But with a family on the way, he could not pursue his dream in sports – Austin Jr. said his father played baseball briefly for the Homestead Grays of the Negro league – and was a supply clerk in the Navy for thirty years.

"I always felt I had to outwork people," the younger Carr said. "I never got to the point – until maybe I started getting college offers at the end of my junior year – that maybe I am starting to get there. It was a constant drive. I never relaxed. There was always that little tension there to compete and be the best."

When it came to basketball, Carr thought he gained an edge on the District playgrounds, always playing with and competing against older players, including those from the professional and college ranks who returned home. That way, when he played against players his own age, Carr had no fear.

Carr made second-team All-Met as a sophomore in 1965 and was first-team the next two years. His senior year, 1966-67, included a memorable 56-51 victory over DeMatha, snapping Mackin's twenty-one game losing streak to the Stags. It was DeMatha's first loss to a local opponent in more than four years.

"That's the way it was [almost] my whole four years: They were Number One and we were Number Two," Carr said. "You talk about frustrating. Our whole year was built on beating them. My junior year, we lost to them twice during the regular season, and I really think we were so dejected after losing to them that we didn't have the same spirit in our games."

As the points and victories kept piling up for Carr and Trojans, college coaches continued to flock to town.

"A coach from Florida State came to see him and he was sitting on the stage with me, watching practice," Furlong said, noting how the Mackin gym was so small that the Trojans never played home games at their school. "After forty-five minutes, he came over and whispered to me, 'Which one is Carr?' Can you believe that? This is his senior year, and he just melted right in."

Furlong had a similar story when the Trojans traveled to Winston-Salem, North Carolina, to play the Wake Forest University freshman team.

Billy Packer, then an assistant coach before going on to a long career as a TV analyst, "set up the game, two years in a row," Furlong said. "The second year, [the Wake Forest freshman team] had beaten the varsity. We beat them by eighteen points. [University of South Carolina Coach] Frank McGuire was at the game. Billy Packer came up to me afterward and said, 'I never noticed Austin during the game and then I picked up the stat sheet and he had thirty-two points, sixteen rebounds and eleven assists.'

"Nobody could cover him. He was great without the ball."

Being in good shape "was part of the game; that was one thing my father taught me," Carr said. "Never let anybody outwork you. You have to be in shape to do that."

Mackin went on to win the Catholic league championship in 1967 and was invited to the Alhambra Catholic Invitational Tournament in Cumberland, Maryland. There, with all the teams staying in the Fort Cumberland Hotel downtown, Austin Carr Sr. sat down to eat breakfast one morning with DeMatha Coach Morgan Wootten and had a surprise for the coach.

"I guess it's a real shame Austin didn't get to play for you," Carr said. "He really wanted to come to DeMatha."

Wootten's ears perked up. He had no idea. He had never heard of Carr until the player began scoring points by the dozen for the Trojans.

"He wanted to play football as well as basketball, and Mackin didn't have football," Carr said. "We called the secretary and she said, 'We are full,' and hung up."

But it worked out well enough for all involved. After Mackin, Carr took his scoring show to Notre Dame, where he led a pack of players from the Washington area and proceeded to rewrite the Fighting Irish record book.

Taken by the Cavaliers with the first overall pick in the 1971 NBA draft, Carr's first few years as a pro were slowed by foot and knee injuries. He played ten seasons in the NBA, the first nine for the Cavaliers, averaging a career-best 21.9 points and 3.8 assists in 1973-74.

"I could shoot the ball, but I played without the ball quite a bit," Carr said. "Most guys that score points don't play without the ball as much as I did. You have to be in constant motion and you have to be in shape. And when your opportunities come, you had to take advantage of them."

13. Walt Williams

Walt Williams was supposed to leave the University of Maryland. He was supposed to transfer. Why would he stay? He had two years of playing eligibility remaining and the Terrapins had been banned from playing in the NCAA tournament in both of those years.

Worse yet, the NCAA barred the Terrapins from having any games televised live during the 1990-91 season; that meant Maryland would not even be allowed to participate in the Atlantic Coast Conference tournament.

No elite player in his right mind – certainly not a six-foot, eight-inch guard/forward/center they called "Wizard" and who had an eye on an NBA career – would stay.

Williams was supposed to pack his bags, thank everyone for the ride while it lasted, give away his Maryland gear and find a new team.

The way NCAA rules were set up, it was as if Williams were a free agent. Unlike other transfers, because of the severe penalties facing Maryland, he would not have to sit out a season at his new school and would be eligible the next season.

Now, in the summer of 1990, two years into his college career, everyone around him was telling him to leave College Park as the NCAA sent the Terrapins to their own little room and shut off the lights as punishment for multiple rules violations under then-coach Bob Wade.

Williams saw it differently.

Yes, after the 1989-90 season, he had gone into a season-ending meeting with Coach Gary Williams and explained how he badly wanted to play in the NCAA tournament – the Terrapins had been on the bubble in March 1990 but not-so-surprisingly passed over given their impending tournament ban – and play in games that were televised. It was not as if NBA scouts could watch games or highlights online back then. Those two things, Walt Williams thought, were vital if he wanted to play in the NBA.

But there were other concerns. Walt Williams had chosen Maryland because it was close to home and it was where the late Len Bias became a star. Sure, Georgetown, Virginia and other schools not too far away were interested in obtaining Williams' services, but none offered the opportunity to follow in his idol's footsteps.

Throughout the summer, Williams said little about his pending decision. Inside, though, there was never really anything to consider.

"The reason I didn't say anything or make a decision early was I thought to myself, 'I should be thinking about going somewhere else, maybe it will come,'" Walt Williams said. "I talked to [Nevada-Las Vegas Coach] Jerry Tarkanian. I talked to the guy at Virginia, [Brian] Ellerbe, who was an assistant coach. I talked to a couple schools: 'Man, I've got to think I should leave one of these days.' But it never happened. I always wanted to be at Maryland. Like I said, I wanted to be Bias. I couldn't be Bias anywhere else but Maryland."

And with that decision, perhaps more than anything else, the Maryland Terrapins were saved from obliteration. Gary Williams thinks it might have saved his job.

"Without Walt [staying] here, I probably would have been gone," Gary Williams said, noting that Williams not only helped the Terrapins achieve success during his playing days but also helped them recruit several talented players.

But Walt Williams never thought a decision about where he would play basketball was that big a deal.

After all, he had gone almost unnoticed throughout his high school career – and in the case of Maryland, he had gone completely unnoticed. Although Williams had blown up during the summer before his senior year at Crossland High in Temple Hills, Maryland – just 20 miles away – it took a phone call from Crossland Coach Earl Hawkins to Maryland's basketball offices to see if Wade was interested in his star.

It must have been a mix-up in the mail! the disbelieving Hawkins was told.

Of course, Walt Williams was so unassuming, he did not care if he was somehow slighted by Wade or Maryland's staff. He had blossomed late and did not follow the same path as most tall teenagers with basketball skills.

Though he was enamored with the game and was always found on a blacktop with a ball in his hands, Williams had played in one organized game before high school. Even when he got to Crossland, basketball was not terribly important; after Williams and a friend got in a fight and were suspended from school for three days, he missed tryouts for the junior varsity team – not that he minded.

The first day of tryouts had consisted of "a lot of running that didn't have to do with basketball," Williams said. "A lot of suicides. I was like, 'Oh, my goodness.'"

"I just loved playing basketball, I didn't care if I was on a team or not. It wasn't that attractive to me to be on the team at that point. It was something I hadn't done before. But I felt it was something I could do."

When the suspension ended, Williams returned to school but the team had been selected. He was unsure what to do. Not knowing anything about how a team is selected, he did not know he could simply tell his parents he had been cut. Instead, he asked to be the team's water boy.

"I didn't know anything about that," Theresa Williams said, more than twenty years after the fact.

Walt Williams apparently performed those duties admirably. Midway through the season, when more than half of the team became academically ineligible, the water boy got a uniform.

"That's how I got a chance to play," he said. "It was a little nerveracking for me. I had never played before an audience."

More important, with his son on the floor, Walter Williams Sr. came to games and made an impression on his son.

"The look on his face after I would play a game made me want to keep playing and drove me to be better than everyone," Walt said.

As a sophomore, Williams made the varsity. He did not start, but that did not matter. Under Hawkins, Crossland was on the verge of a dynasty.

The Cavaliers won the only state championship in school history that season, then made it to the state final the next two seasons. Crossland beat Whitman, 64-59, for the 1986 Maryland AA title, then lost 73-69, to Northwestern High and standout Jay Bias, Len's younger brother, in the 1987 final.

Along the way, Williams went from water boy to reserve to starter to full-blown superstar, playing a myriad of positions as he grew to six-seven.

However, perhaps the most important game Williams ever played during high school was not in Maryland or in a Crossland uniform.

In July 1987, before his senior year, Williams had been invited to the prestigious Five-Star basketball camp in Pittsburgh. It was the first time he had flown on an airplane. The only trips he had been on were to family reunions in Dunn, North Carolina, or amusement parks such as Kings Dominion or family vacations to such places as the Pocono Mountains in northeastern Pennsylvania.

"It was a little different for me, but of course I was of the age I couldn't show it," Williams said. "I had to play off that I could handle it. But I was scared to death.

"I was battling all types of things on that trip. I had never been away from my folks. First trip flying. Being away from home, especially for an extensive period like a week. Playing against top players in the nation. I had never experienced anything like that. I was used to playing people from around the way and schools we played. That was a new experience."

Many of the other players also seemed to know one another. Williams, quietly, followed them around – to the dorms, to the cafeteria, to the gym. In the mid-to-late 1980s, summer camps were a small part of the basketball scene, a universe away from the seemingly nonstop series of events for today's high school players. Forget the immediacy of reports on the Internet; maybe there would be a newsletter write-up a few weeks out.

"I felt out of place until we started playing basketball," he said. "That's when I started to feel comfortable."

Unbeknownst to her son, after dropping him off at National Airport, Theresa Williams called the camp daily to check on him.

"He was gone for a week -- that was pretty scary for us," she said. "I don't think he ever knew I did that. I just called to see how he was doing."

Anxious to see where he stood – Hawkins had advised him of the high talent level at the camp – Williams exceeded any expectations after leading his team to a victory over uber-touted Alonzo Mourning's team in the championship game. Williams and Mourning were matched up at both ends of the court, with the six-seven, one hundred sixty-five pound Williams guarding the nearly seven-foot Mourning. Afterward, as he walked back to the dorm, Williams heard someone yelling to him.

It was Five-Star organizer Howard Garfinkel, who had been following Williams the whole way from the gym without being able to get his attention.

"That's the first time Alonzo has ever lost at this camp," Garfinkel said.

Williams had not grasped the significance of the victory. He knew that Mourning, Billy Owens and Stanley Roberts were among the top players, but little more.

"I had no clue who any of these guys were, but he made me quickly realize the magnitude of what I had done," Williams said. "That made me have a lot more confidence. It let me know I could compete against anybody in the country that I played against."

It also alerted colleges that Walt Williams might be worthy of their attention. Soon the recruiting letters started to pile up.

The first came from Penn State. Then Colgate. St. Bonaventure. Wake Forest. North Carolina did not send a letter, but Tar Heels Coach Dean Smith attended a Crossland practice. So did Villanova Coach Rollie Massimino.

"Then I started to know that maybe I could play in college," Williams said.

Theresa Williams was particularly impressed by Smith and the way he said he checked up on her son.

"He told me that he and his coaches didn't talk just to coaches, that he and his people talk to the teachers and janitors to see what they have to say," she said. "And he said that everybody had nothing but great things to say about" Walt Williams.

Noticeably absent among the schools beginning to recruit Williams was Maryland. So Hawkins got on the phone.

Yes, the Terrapins were interested.

"That was all I needed to hear," Williams said. "Growing up, I was a big Georgetown fan. What turned me into a Maryland fan was Len Bias. You know back then, John Thompson and the Hoyas were everything. By the time I got to that level at high school, I started watching Maryland and started watching Bias and I wanted to be him. More than anything. I couldn't be Bias at Georgetown. I could kill two birds with one stone. I could still be in the crib and I wanted to be Bias."

Williams had played one game with Bias at the old lighted courts on the south hill at College Park. He had gone over to campus with his older sister Stephanie, who was a student at Maryland, the first member of the family to go to college. While waiting for his sister to return home, Walt watched a pickup game.

"They needed one [more player] and I just happened to be out there," Williams said. "I was on Bias' team. I always had high tops on, but I played in anything – church shoes, whatever. I remember we won, but after that I had to go. I don't think I touched the ball, I was just running up and down the court. I just couldn't believe it."

Williams went through with a few official campus visits as courtesies to the coaches recruiting him, but they were unnecessary. Before preseason practice started his senior year, Williams told Hawkins to let Maryland know he would accept its scholarship offer, before he even told his parents.

"My mother was upset about that; she was upset she wasn't the first one I told," Williams said. "I didn't look at it as that big a deal. I just knew where I was going. She was happy I was going to be at home though."

Williams' senior year was a blast. The Cavaliers rolled through the regular season undefeated. In the playoffs, Williams had twenty-seven of his thirty-one points in the first half of an 85-63 blowout of Gaithersburg in the state semifinals, setting up a rematch against Springbrook in the championship game. Crossland entered 25-0, but it was 25-1 Springbrook that pulled out the victory despite Williams' game-high twenty-four points.

After averaging 22.3 points – slightly behind teammate Bernard Hunt's 22.7 per game average -- Williams was named first-team All-Met.

"In Hawk's offense, I was out on the wing, but sometimes he'd run isolations for me," Williams said. "I got to do it all. I just wanted to be on the court, I did not care" what position.

While Williams's final three seasons at Crossland were relatively smooth sailing, his time at Maryland could not have been any more tumultuous.

Wade was forced to resign after Williams's freshman season in the wake of an NCAA investigation that revealed he had provided improper benefits to players and then misstated his role to investigators. During Williams's sophomore year in 1989-90, as he began to emerge as an elite player in the college game, the NCAA levied penalties that it has not since come close to matching.

The punishment was too much for Jerrod Mustaf; the former DeMatha Catholic High star skipped his final two years of eligibility to turn professional.

Gary Williams thought that Walt Williams – not quite ready for the NBA – would transfer to a school that would help him achieve his goal of making it to the NBA. So the coach responded with the pitch that the Wizard could play all over the court and would be such an integral part of the team that no other team could offer such an opportunity.

"He has Bias's game. He could do a lot of things," Gary Williams said. "Bias was a good perimeter shooter. One thing I thought Walt was better at was putting the ball on the floor. Bias was probably a little better athlete than Walt. Bias by the time he was a junior at Maryland was Superman. He could do things a lot of guys couldn't do."

Although not quite Superman, Williams was a darn good Wizard. He had played small forward as a freshman and point guard as a sophomore.

His junior year, though, was cut short by a fractured left fibula that had him miss the bulk of the Atlantic Coast Conference season. As a senior, though, Walt Williams made second-team All-American. He scored thirty or more points in seven consecutive ACC games, a feat that has not been matched since. He was selected seventh overall in the 1992 NBA draft by the Sacramento Kings.

One night after being drafted, Walt and his future wife April were driving down Lottsford Road in Landover in his new, green BMW 525, when she turned down the radio and asked a question.

"Did you ever think you would be in the NBA?" she said.

"Yeah, this is amazing," Walt replied. "I can't believe that."

Williams played eleven years in the NBA, averaging in double figures in scoring seven times, including a career-high seventeen points per game as a rookie.

Living outside of Olney, Maryland, Walt and April have three sons: Walt, Kamari and Bryce. Walt coaches the boys on their basketball teams and analyzes Terrapins' basketball games on the radio.

12. Johnny Dawkins

Johnny Dawkins always was the one organizing a basketball game or gathering his friends and teammates at one of their favorites courts. Occasionally, though, the games found him.

Picture this: It is an afternoon in June and Dawkins is getting ready to head to a graduation party for a friend of his girlfriend's when the phone rings in the Dawkins house in Rockville. On the other end of the line? Former All-Met and college Player of the Year Adrian Dantley, who had averaged thirty points per game for the second consecutive season for the NBA's Utah Jazz – calling to tell Dawkins where and when to meet for that day's game.

"Wherever I was, I pretty much dropped what I was doing and grabbed my gear," said Dawkins, who as a star at Mackin High in the early 1980s became a regular offseason practice partner for Dantley, Duck Williams, Jo Jo Hunter and other standouts.

"But this one time, I wasn't going to do it. I remember my father hearing me tell Dantley and those guys I wasn't going to do it. That didn't go over too well."

Before the teenager got off the phone, Johnny Dawkins Sr. had altered his son's plans.

"I'll be there," the younger Dawkins said before hanging up.

For an energetic high schooler, the opportunity to play with professional stars in the prime of their career could not be passed up. It was a key part of Dawkins' basketball education, often playing one-on-one or two-on-two fullcourt.

"That helped me as much as anything," Dawkins said. "Those guys are great players. Having them take my lunch – I can remember one summer losing every single game and I'm getting on the bus to go home thinking I'll never be a good player.

"I had two choices: Sink or swim. That's what it does to you. Fortunately, I was able to swim."

Dawkins was no average swimmer. He will go down as one of the finest shooters ever from the Washington area, having starred at Mackin and Duke University before a nine-year NBA career during which he averaged 11.1 points and 5.5 assists per game. He then went into coaching and, after ten years as an assistant at Duke, in 2008 was hired as the head coach at Stanford University.

The son of a Metro bus driver and a social worker, Johnny Dawkins always was interested in basketball. His father and four uncles played nearly every weekend, and young Johnny liked to tag along and occasionally would get to play.

"Seeing that excited me about the game," said Dawkins, who has a younger brother, James. "Watching them go play and compete."

As he grew older and started to become a player, it was Dawkins who was out the door looking for a game. He'd call friends from Mackin or other schools and arrange that day's game.

"We'd go court to court in those days, there weren't many gyms like there are now," said childhood friend Kelvin Johnson, who played at DeMatha High, where Dawkins nearly was his teammate. "Candy Cane, Sligo, Hillandale, Fort Stevens, the University of Maryland – anywhere we could find a good basketball game."

"That's what we did back then," said Dawkins, who also pushed friends and teammates to lift weights with him in his basement before going out to play. "Wherever you could go and compete, you did."

As a youngster, Dawkins lived in Northwest Washington, just down the street from Coolidge High, and often played over at Takoma, Fort Stevens or Paul Junior High. He met many of his close friends through CYO basketball; Dawkins played for Nativity. His seventh-grade team also included future NFL players Joe Howard and Chris Pike. The Dawkins family moved to Rockville in 1978, before Johnny's freshman year of high school. He had anticipated going to DeMatha, and attended summer school there before the ninth grade.

"Up until the week before [school started], I'm ready to go to DeMatha," Dawkins said. "It just so happened my mom got my tuition in late, she didn't pay it on time. So my spot was taken.

"I tried to look at several other schools – Carroll, Gonzaga and a few others – but at that late date, no school is really available. Everybody was full with the kids they have coming in. I was very fortunate that Mackin had that open spot. At the time, I didn't know very much about the school. I knew it had a good basketball tradition. As did DeMatha. But other than that, I didn't know too much about it.

"I tell you what, though, it was the best thing that could have happened to me. It couldn't have worked out any better, the experience I had going to that school."

Indeed, Mackin had one of the city's top basketball programs, with such alumni as Austin Carr, Hunter and Williams. The Trojans had well-documented problems when it came to beating DeMatha – "That drove me crazy. That still bothers me to this day," Dawkins said -- but otherwise they were among the city's elite.

Dawkins played on the freshman team as a freshman and "was praying I could maybe make the varsity as a sophomore." Mackin Coach Steve Hocker took an assistant coaching job at Providence College, but he called Dawkins aside and told him not to transfer, that he had a bright future at Mackin.

The new coach, Paul DeStefano, kept Dawkins on the varsity but initially brought him off the bench, wanting to give the team's juniors and seniors first crack at the starting lineup.

"We played in the O'Connell Christmas tournament, which was one of the best tournaments around, and he started in that tournament," DeStefano said. "He had a great, great tournament. We lost in the finals to Holy Trinity from Long Island. Matt Doherty was on that team, Bob McKillop [now the head coach at Davidson College] was the coach. He started the rest of his career."

Dawkins averaged fourteen points that sophomore year, but made his biggest strides in the next summer and went from being a player to being the leader. Playing against DeMatha in the Jelleff League semifinals, the front-row crowd included North Carolina Coach Dean Smith, Duke Coach Mike Krzyzewski, North Carolina State Coach Jim Valvano and Georgetown Coach John Thompson, among others.

"I think the score at halftime was 57-53," said DeStefano, who has had a lengthy coaching career. "DeMatha had [Adrian] Branch. They were very, very good. We ended up losing, but it was a show. It was really a show."

And Dawkins realized that he was one of the stars.

"That's when I started to turn the corner and started to realize things I was about to do to the fullest – I was a good player, but how I really could impact the game," Dawkins said.

It was around that time that Dantley, Hunter, Williams and others started pulling Dawkins into their circle. And what better teacher than Dantley, whose work ethic was revered by the other players?

"He was the first guy I've ever seen who really showed me how to work," Dawkins said. "I was always going to play. If there's a game, five-on-five or whatever, I'm in, wherever. But he was the guy who showed me how to work on shooting, work on ballhandling."

Not that Dantley drilled Dawkins on what to do or how to play. It was simply instructing by example.

"I'd watch him before we played one-on-ones and I'd pick up those traits," Dawkins said. "The next thing I know, I'm doing it too."

Sometimes Dawkins would get the call several times a week to join the pros' game. Then he might go a few weeks without hearing from them.

"It depended on their schedules, they were professionals. Whenever I got the call, I was going to be there," Dawkins said. "I was excited to compete with them. Those guys were doing what I eventually wanted to do. As a competitor, you want to go up against the best.

"There was definitely some gratitude. I was thankful they let me play. They must have seen something in me to let me play. I learned so many things from those guys. I took my lumps. But I took my lumps on the playground, too. I wasn't always the best player."

But by his final two years of high school, Dawkins was among the best. As a junior, the smooth left-handed shooter averaged 24.3 points, scored at least thirty points in eight games and made first-team All-Met. That summer, he was the only high schooler selected by Thompson to the East Region team in the National Sports Festival, which only helped his growing confidence and strengthened his resolve to work out and get better.

"Once he gained the confidence, his game went to another level," Johnson said.

"Everything I did, I put a lot of time in the gym," Dawkins said. "I've had guys tell me I was crazy, 'Can't believe you're up there, shooting and working out,' while guys were doing other things. I had that commitment. I had a dream a long time ago that I wanted to play in the NBA.

"You have to work at it, but you have to be blessed, too. To me, there were some great players, terrific players, who were better than I was and didn't make it. How do you account for those things? There are so many things that can trip you up. You talk about the classroom. You talk about the things off the court. You talk about injuries. It has to fall right for you."

By his senior year at Mackin in 1981-82, everything was falling into place for Dawkins. Again, he excelled on the court and repeated as a first-team All-Met, though Linwood Davis of Theodore Roosevelt and Michael Jackson of South Lakes shared The Washington Post's Player of the Year honors. The Post said of Dawkins:

First-team all-Met last year . . . averaged 22 points a game, mostly on classic 20-foot jumpers . . . good first step to get open and is accurate from long range . . .has good percentages from floor and free throw line . . . plays good defense and jumps well . . .long arms and deceptive speed are assets.

A few weeks later, Dawkins committed to play for Duke, choosing the Blue Devils over Georgetown, Maryland and Notre Dame.

"Anytime I had a game, Duke had a presence, they were there," Dawkins said. "It showed a heck of a commitment. That didn't seal the deal, but it did leave an impression. The ultimate impression is spending time with the coach and developing a relationship during the recruiting process."

As much as he excelled on the court, Dawkins still did not always look the part. The summer before he enrolled at Duke, soon-to-be classmate Jay Bilas was a little surprised when he met Dawkins. Bilas, a six-eight forward from Southern California, was visiting Washington with his parents. He decided to spend an afternoon playing basketball with Dawkins.

The Bilases drove out to Rockville and Jay knocked on the door of the Dawkins home.

"Uh, is your brother home?" Jay asked the skinny kid who answered the door.

"No, he's not," Johnny said, introducing himself before taking Jay down to Hillandale for a game.

"When they picture some of the things you do out there or how you play, they look for someone a lot bigger," Dawkins said.

Coming off a 10-17 season in 1981-82, Duke struggled similarly the next season, finishing 11-17 after a 109-66 loss to Virginia in the Atlantic Coast Conference tournament quarterfinals.

"That freshman year was very disappointing to all of us," said forward David Henderson, who roomed with Dawkins their final three years at Duke. "We made a pact at the end of our freshman year that would never happen again. [The loss to Virginia] was embarrassing. Virginia never beat us again in our career."

Duke won eighty percent of its games the next three seasons, culminating in a run to the NCAA championship game in 1986, where the Blue Devils lost to Louisville, 72-69. Dawkins averaged 20.2 points per game that season and was named the Naismith College Player of the Year.

Dawkins, who had been an alternate for the 1984 U.S. Olympic team, was selected with the tenth pick by the San Antonio Spurs in that summer's NBA draft. He played three seasons for the Spurs, five for the Philadelphia 76ers and one for the Detroit Pistons before retiring in 1995.

One year later, he returned to Duke with aspirations of becoming a college athletic director. But after two seasons working as an intern in a variety of positions in his alma mater's athletic department, in 1998 Dawkins moved to the coaching staff, filling the vacancy created when Tommy Amaker became the head coach at Seton Hall. After passing on several opportunities to interview and become a head coach, Dawkins took over at Stanford in 2008.

Coaching "is truly what I believe I was meant to do," Dawkins said. "I never had a day of work doing it. Everyday has been a great day. I love what I do. That's a labor of love. You get to work with young people, help develop them and mold them."

As for the girlfriend whose friend's party he skipped? Johnny and Tracy now have four grown children.

11. Dennis Scott

Looking back, thirty years later, Dennis Scott might have been the player who changed Washington-area high school basketball forever.

In the summer of 1983, Scott was the tallest fourteen-year-old around. He had just finished his freshman year at Loudoun County High School in Leesburg, Virginia. The six-foot, seven-inch Scott started at center for the Raiders, but Coach Jim Parker allowed the blossoming ninth-grader to play wherever he needed.

Thirty miles to the southeast, Stu Vetter was still a relative youngster in the coaching business, at tiny Flint Hill School in Oakton. He had mutton chops, wore plaid jackets and went by Stewart.

But then Vetter persuaded Scott to transfer to Flint Hill. The player would have to repeat his freshman year -- partly to adapt to the private school's academic system, but he also would benefit athletically. Although public schools generally limit students to four years of athletic eligibility, Flint Hill was not a member of the Virginia High School League or any conference. If Scott wanted to repeat a year of school – a practice now commonly known as reclassifying – so be it.

Adding to the confluence of events, one year earlier USA Today came into existence and began compiling its national high school football and basketball rankings. With Scott and a host of other talented players, there was an avenue for Vetter's budding squad to receive prime-time recognition.

At times during Scott's final two seasons at Flint Hill, the Falcons were USA Today's top-ranked team.

"The reason Flint Hill became known was Dennis Scott," Vetter said. "And timing. No one thought that USA Today poll was going to last -- it was 'McPaper.' But because of the timing Flint Hill got known pretty quickly. From that point on, we started getting the George Lynches and Randolph Childresses."

Sure enough, Flint Hill gained a national reputation, attracting a wide range of talented players. Vetter's profile rose considerably. More players saw the athletic benefits of an extra year of high school.

All because of the skinny teenager whose parents used to carry a birth certificate to youth-league games to quiet complaints that the superstar player was a ringer who was too old.

Vetter, of course, has had national-caliber programs at Flint Hill; Harker Prep in Potomac, Maryland; St. John's/Prospect Hall in Frederick, Maryland; and at Montrose Christian School in Rockville, Maryland. Morgan Wootten might be the only coach in the Naismith Memorial Basketball Hall of Fame solely because of his contributions to high school basketball, but after thirty-six seasons on the sidelines Vetter will be part of the debate about who is the Washington area's most successful basketball coach of all-time.

And Scott?

He might have been tall, but boy could he shoot! He went on to a sensational career as part of Georgia Tech's Lethal Weapon 3 with Kenny Anderson and Brian Oliver. He was the fourth overall pick in the 1990 NBA draft and played ten years in the league, making his mark as one of the finest three-point shooters ever.

"He is one of the best pure shooters in high school I've ever seen," Vetter said. "To this day, I don't think I've coached a better pure shooter or seen a better pure shooter. He didn't have everything else. But Dennis could sit right there in the stands with his wrist and hit it.

"If we had the three-[point shot] back then, everybody would have recognized what a great shooter he was. Every shot he took pretty much was a three, but we only got two points! The three-point shot came in the next year. I went back and looked at some of the tapes and I'd say, 'Man, we would have won that game no problem'" if Scott's long-distance baskets had counted for three points.

Consider that in college, when Georgia Tech played the University of Maryland, Terrapins Coach Gary Williams ordered his players to get out and defend Scott at any cost, anywhere on the court.

"Every time he caught it, the guy guarding him had the job to make him put it on the floor," Williams said. "It didn't matter whether he went by you. He had range."

In the NBA, playing his first seven seasons with the Orlando Magic, Scott set league records for most three-pointers in a game (eleven) and in a season (267).

Not too shabby for the oh-so-tall kid from Hagerstown, Maryland.

He was the second of two children born to Elizabeth and Dennis E. Scott Sr. A brother, Eldon Brown, is eight years older. When Elizabeth and Dennis Sr. divorced, she took the younger Dennis back to Northern Virginia, where he was an all-around athlete.

"I played football and basketball all the way up to seventh grade. Then finally I let the Pop Warner stuff go," he said. "My older son found my Punt, Pass and Kick trophies from when I was nine years old, ten years old, eleven years old. And he said, 'What the hell do you know?' And I told him, 'The trophy doesn't lie.'"

Scott, a first baseman or outfielder on the baseball diamond, had given up that sport because it moved too slow. It was during his time at J. Lupton Simpson Middle School that he stopped playing football and focused on basketball. Then he became the first freshman to start every game at Loudoun County High, helping the Raiders beat an Osbourn Park Yellow Jackets team led by David Robinson in the playoffs.

"Coach said, 'You're going to start at center, but you're going to play all five positions,'" Scott said. "He was one of the first coaches to let me get a rebound and just bring it up the court. Of course, I was growing up watching Magic Johnson play, and then people were opening up their eyes to letting big guys bring the ball up the court."

But while Scott played well for the Raiders, former middle school classmate Brian Domalik wanted Scott to join him at Flint Hill. Domalik had gone to play for Vetter straight out of middle school, he and his parents deciding that it was worth the daily trek to play for the Falcons.

"Dennis and I were so close, and he was being recruited by Flint Hill and DeMatha at the same time," Domalik said. "I think it came down to the fact that he and I were so close that he decided to go to Flint Hill."

Of course, that created a mild uproar in Leesburg.

"When they heard I might be transferring, you look back now, but it was like LeBron [James] leaving Cleveland," Scott said. "At the time, in 1983, things were not like they are now – where you can stay in a small-market school and get the exposure you need and coaches see you play. ... Going to Hawaii four years in a row, going to Vegas, the Virgin Islands, all the Christmas and holiday tournaments we went to -- it prepares you better for college than a public school setting."

Getting to Flint Hill was not easy.

Scott would wake up at five-thirty a.m., and usually ate an egg-and-cheese sandwich while his mother made the short drive to the intersection of U.S. 15 and Virginia State Road 7, where he would catch a ride with Domalik to Flint Hill.

"On a good day, it might take us an hour to an hour and a half to get to school," Scott said. "On the way home, it was an hour and a half to two hours."

When the academic day ended around three p.m., there usually was study hall and then Vetter's basketball class got started.

"By the time I got to college, the routine and study and discipline were embedded," Scott said. "So getting up and going to class wasn't hard."

As for needing to repeat his freshman year, Scott said he simply was following direction from the adults around him. Born September 5, 1968, he had started school at five years old. Staying back one year would not make him significantly older than his classmates.

"I trusted the system because I had seen other kids do it and thought this may be the route to go," Scott said. "For me, [transferring] was tough at first because the school was so small. That was the real adjustment. But it was an advantage. Instead of being in a class with fifty kids, I was in a class with eleven kids. The chance to not pay attention or the temptation to talk in class or make remarks in class, those were gone. A public school system, when you get out of school, you may go to a store or hang out in the hall, but at Flint Hill it was go to your locker, change your clothes and go to study hall.

"You figured out quickly what the system was."

Basketball had always come naturally for Scott, and that did not change.

"Shooting came easy," he said. "I realized everybody could dunk, but no one could really knock down consistent outside shots as a kid."

Except Scott.

His teammate always had exceptional hand-eye coordination, Domalik said, dating back to when they played on all-star teams during sixth, seventh and eighth grades and traveled around Northern Virginia beating other all-star squads.

"We never lost a game, I don't think anybody came close to beating us," Domalik said. "Mostly because Dennis was so good. I think he could dunk a basketball when he was in seventh grade. Of course, that was just incredible. He was a man amongst boys.

"We played in a little small town in Leesburg, and everybody went to the community center to play and there were really good players. And he was playing with the best kids, the biggest kids since he was in the sixth grade. And he was always one of the best players."

So when Scott arrived at Flint Hill for the 1983-84 season, it only made sense that he was one of the Falcons' best players. Darrick Simms was the leader, but Scott was not far behind. He had fifteen points and eight rebounds in one of his first games, an 86-60 victory over the Central Falcons.

As a sophomore, Scott scored seventeen points when Flint Hill beat USA Today's top-ranked Mercer Island Islanders, 60-56, in a tournament in Las Vegas. Beating the team from suburban Seattle, led by Brian Schwade and Quin Snyder, was "the greatest win in the school's history," Vetter told The Washington Post at the time.

Scott made third-team All-Met that year. As a junior, Flint Hill lost one game, 58-57, in overtime to Oak Hill as Scott fouled out after scoring twelve points. The loss prevented the Falcons from finished No. 1 in USA Today, but they finished atop The Washington Post rankings. Scott made first-team All-Met, having averaged 22.5 points, 8.8 rebounds and 5.1 assists while earning most valuable player honors in four tournaments.

As a senior, Scott averaged twenty-four points, 11.4 rebounds, 6.6 assists and 3.5 steals as the Falcons went 23-0. He was named All-Met Player of the Year.

Then it came time to choose a college.

Although his son Ronny played for Flint Hill, Georgetown Hoyas Coach John Thompson never offered a scholarship to Scott. Like many Washington-area teenagers, Scott thought he would play for the Maryland Terrapins.

"I was going to Maryland before the Len Bias situation," Scott said. Bias died after Scott's junior year ended. "I had the route down on how I could drive around [Interstate] 495 to get home on the weekend. Keith Gatlin is a good friend to this day. And when Lefty [Driesell] was at Georgia State, I used to go to games -- that's how cool we were."

Scott similarly liked Bobby Cremins, the Georgia Tech coach. Cremins was a tireless recruiter, so it was not much of a surprise that he was in a Fairfax hotel room pursuing the prospect when Scott called to let the coach know he had made his choice.

"I'm one of those personalities, 'Don't B.S. me and I won't B.S. you.' And that's how Bobby is," Scott said. "He said, 'Dennis, if you don't go to class, you're going to be up at six o'clock every morning and you're not going to play.' The second week of the season, I missed my eight a.m. class. The next day, the academic advisor took me to the track and made sure I ran the mile."

Scott did not have to beat any set time. Just being on the track, running instead of sleeping in the predawn hours, was enough to get the message across.

Once he figured things out at Georgia Tech, Scott was a star, solidifying his place as an elite outside shooter. He was the Atlantic Coast Conference Player of the Year as a junior in 1989-90, leading the Yellow Jackets to the NCAA Tournament Final Four.

"I didn't think about [playing] in the NBA until the Final Four run, didn't think about it one bit," Scott said. "Then people started talking about it. People were coming up to me. I tell the media, a lot of times you do the homework for the player. The worst anyone saw me going was five and I ended up going four. The rest is history."

Indeed, Scott was drafted by the Orlando Magic, where his long-range shooting continued. He was a career 39.7 percent shooter from three-point range, setting records for most three-pointers in a season (267) and in a game (eleven), though those marks have since been broken. His last NBA season was in 1999-2000.

Scott now works for as an analyst on NBA TV. He and his wife, Rachael, have four children.

10. George Leftwich

In some ways, George Leftwich was ahead of his time. After all, attending three high schools in one year, then repeating his sophomore year at a fourth school would blend in with the way many top contemporary basketball players get an education. And when he played, graduating from Archbishop Carroll High in 1960, Leftwich and teammates were ahead of their time, too. The Lions were one of the greatest high school teams ever in the Washington area, winning fifty-five consecutive games. They were also among the first racially integrated teams in a city where race had long been a dividing line.

"It was a very different experience," Leftwich said. "You've got to remember now, all my life I'd been in all-black situations. Schools were segregated. It was different. And I didn't even know what Catholicism was."

More than fifty years later, Leftwich can still recount how a naïve teenager ended up at an admissions interview hoping to get into the private school near the crest of the hill off North Capitol Street in Northeast Washington.

He had grown up on Thirteenth Street, Northwest. The youngest of three children born to Willie and Maude Leftwich, George always was a good athlete and possessed a strong work ethic. Occasionally, the two collided, such as the time ten-year-old George tried to talk his mother into buying him some sneakers.

"I wanted to get a pair of Chuck Taylors then," he said. "All I knew was the good players wore the shoes with the red stripes on them, around the sole, the Converse All-Stars, I didn't know the name. My mother wanted to get me the U.S. Keds with the real thick rubber gum sole. She thought they would last longer. They were three dollars and the Chucks were five. But that was the budget."

The young boy found a solution to the problem, taking a newspaper route delivering The Washington Post.

"That's a lost art," Leftwich said. "You know what I learned? You've got to work every day -- rain, snow or shine. My father wasn't going to [deliver newpapers for him] and my older brother [Willie Jr.] served them, too. I think I got a work ethic from that. I owe that to The Washington Post."

Leftwich also had discipline, an attribute for which he credited his father. Willie Leftwich supported his family by working two jobs, driving for Eastside Cab and attending to baggage for the American Association of Railroads. Other than going to nearby Monroe Elementary School, George was not allowed off the square block in which the Leftwich family lived. Even when Willie Leftwich would be gone for three or four days on a train to Chicago and back, George did not dare violate that rule.

"He had that much control," George said.

Not that George complained about being limited to a relatively small amount of space. He was allowed in the alley behind the Leftwich house, where he spent countless hours shooting into big peach baskets that he tied to a fence.

"I wore a couple of them out," Leftwich said. "I didn't know the height of the basket. All I knew was it should be up high. I went out there and shot every day. You've got to remember, I still played baseball and football. I was an athlete, I just didn't have the basketball touch."

That had changed by the time Leftwich enrolled at Banneker Junior High, where he was the only eighth-grader to make the basketball team. One of the tallest boys in his grade, always standing in the back of the line, he also was an excellent football player and could play baseball, too. Being such a good athlete, he occasionally tried to sneak something past a teacher or other adult but rarely was successful.

"I thought I could get away with a few things," he said. "But I got away with nothing but a soft behind! I wasn't going to tell my father I did enough to get spanked, or I would get beat again."

As George got older, his father's geographic restrictions softened.

"Once I got to junior high, he started relaxing a little bit when he found out I wasn't going to get in trouble," he said.

Of course, relaxing curfews and trusting your son to meet his end of the bargain are two different things. The first night George was allowed to attend a party, he came home to a surprise.

"He said be home by twelve and I came up the stairs at eleven forty-five," Leftwich said, chuckling. "Guess where he was? In my bed, sleeping, so he would know when I got home."

By the time he was ready for high school, Leftwich had developed into a quite a point guard. He played against older boys on the playgrounds and held his own, building confidence for playing against competition his own age.

"Wil Jones used to work at the Park View playground. He got me on with the big guys -- they called me 'Young Boy,'" Leftwich said. "First time I got on, they fouled me and I said, 'Foul!' They said, 'You can't have the ball because you can't beat anybody.' They pushed me, they hit me – they didn't try to hurt me. After a while, I guess they figured out they weren't going to run me home."

The Cardozo High basketball coach, Frank Bolden, tried to persuade Leftwich to attend his school and play for the Clerks, but Leftwich was not interested. After his family moved into the Coolidge High attendance zone, Leftwich started tenth grade there.

But after a few weeks, he did not like it and transferred to Dunbar, "where all my friends were."

However, a short time later and before the basketball season began, Bolden went to D.C. Public Schools administrators and alleged that neither Leftwich nor sophomore center Tom Hoover, another basketball standout, should be attending Dunbar. Hoover, it turned out, belonged at Theodore Roosevelt High.

"We would have won the city championship every year with both of us in there," Hoover said. "That's why Frank turned us in."

Leftwich then enrolled at McKinley Tech, which at the time could take any student because it was a technical school. (This was before D.C. Public Schools allowed students to enroll at any school operating at less than full capacity.) Hoover went to Carroll, where he joined the basketball team, but Leftwich did not play that season.

"I didn't have a choice. I had to leave Dunbar, which might have been one of the best things that happened," Leftwich said. "Dunbar wasn't exactly what it was ten or fifteen years beforehand. It was turning into a hoodlum school."

Having finished his sophomore year at McKinley, Leftwich soon was on the hunt for a new school. Another boy in his neighborhood, Willie Wells, tried to convince Leftwich that Carroll would be a good fit. But when he went for an interview at the school, it didn't go swimmingly.

"I'm ninety days removed from a segregated system and I'm not Catholic," Leftwich said. "And the only other person I knew was Tom Hoover, who had the distinction of being in more trouble than anybody at Carroll, past or present. ... I didn't even know what Catholicism was. Funny story, in my interview, with Father Burnell, who had this big Beowulfian voice, I'm being very polite and trying to say the right thing and everything is 'Yes, sir.' And he erupts, 'Yes, Faaather!' You would have thought I cursed at him."

Burnell agreed to admit Leftwich, with one condition. Because Leftwich had not done much classwork the previous season, he had to repeat the tenth grade.

Leftwich agreed and, unknowingly, the Lions had themselves a first-rate point guard, though even he was unsure of his role. "I figured the only way to make the team was to outshoot everybody," he said. "And I did."

Carroll rolled out quite a lineup. Monk Malloy was the shooting guard. Hoover, at six-feet, ten-inches, ruled the paint. (John Thompson became a key player the next year.) Walt Skinner was a tough defender.

"George set the tone for the rest of us," said Malloy, who went on to be the president of the University of Notre Dame for eighteen years. "We all had things we did well, and he was able to bring that out from those of us on the starting team. During the time we played together, I think George was the key to the success of the Carroll program.

"Obviously, we had an unusually tall team for that era. We were very balanced in the set of skills that we had. It was difficult for the high school opponents to figure out how to try to beat us. They tried everything from a total slowdown to a box-and-one to every kind of defense you could think up.

"We had a strong inside presence. I was the distant shooter. They could press us, but [George] would beat the press and by the time the ball got downcourt we got easy layups. ... Hoover in some ways was a child in a man's body. He was just a dominating rebounder and shot blocker who could also score."

On one occasion, DeMatha Coach Morgan Wootten decided to double-team Leftwich. Sixth man Billy Barnes, who coached the Lions for five years in the 1970s, then hit three consecutive shots.

"That was the end of that," Barnes said.

While Thompson was the one who later gained national attention for his tough stances while coaching at Georgetown, everyone agreed that Hoover was the Lions' tough guy.

"There was a ne'er-to-do-well from our neighborhood who, after the St. John's-Carroll championship football game my senior year [in November 1958] came up and said something, and Tom slugged him and knocked him out," Malloy said. "The following summer, I was on the playground for some reason and Tom happened to be there with a sport jacket on and the guy came up. He had been drunk the first time and said, 'See if you can take me down now.' Just the two of them. In three or four punches, [Hoover] knocked him out again. This guy was a tough, bully type."

Leftwich knew this from experience. At a practice during that 1957-58 basketball season, the two went up for a rebound and an errant Hoover elbow broke Leftwich's nose. On all other occasions, though, Leftwich appreciated having Hoover around.

"Tom had a big heart; he fancied himself as our big brother," Leftwich said. "He beat the crap out of us upstairs [Carroll's gym is on the school's second floor] but guess what? Nobody else touched us. What could George Leftwich do against a six-five, six-six guy if he wanted to fight? Jump behind Tom. Tom would rather hit you than ask you to move out of his way."

In March 1958, Carroll advanced to the City Title Game before losing to finish the season 28-4. "We lost to Frank Bolden and Cardozo, of all people," Leftwich said. The final score was 67-62. "The worst part of that loss that still sticks with me is we beat them by [64-43] upstairs."

Carroll got payback the next season, beating Cardozo, 79-52, in the City Title Game. The Lions then won the Knights of Columbus Tournament at Georgetown and the Eastern States Catholic Invitational in Newport, R.I.. They finished 33-2 (21-0 against high school opponents), winning their final twenty-four games. Leftwich, after making second-team All-Metropolitan as a sophomore, made the first team as a junior and again as a senior.

Perhaps more important, Carroll's players learned a lesson that while whites and blacks could play together in Washington, when they left the city some folks weren't quite as accepting.

During the Eastern States Catholic tournament, the Lions at one point had five black players on the court.

"What is this, the Harlem Globetrotters?" Leftwich remembers one fan yelling from the stands.

Even in the District, things weren't always easy. One time during a game against visiting Cardozo – with a roster of Leftwich's former teammates from Banneker Junior High -- Leftwich was shooting free throws when an opponent taunted: "You're over here with all these white guys, you must think you're white now, too."

There also was a trip to St. Joseph's to play the Hawks' freshman team. On the way home, the team stopped in Delaware for dinner. After being seated, the players waited. And waited. And waited.

"After twenty or twenty-five minutes, Father [Joe] Duffy went in the back and asked what was going on," Leftwich said. "He never said it, but when he came out he said, 'Fellas, we're going to go down the road and eat.' Those were some of the first racial smacks in the face. He handled it really well."

Said Hoover: "We played in a very difficult time period. ... We were the 'Titans' because we were the first integrated team in the city. A lot of people didn't like it. All those other schools were white. ... The only way [DeMatha Coach Morgan] Wootten got all the black guys was my coach left [and went to St. Anselm's].

"Unless you went through it, you can tell people but they won't know the difference. It was a real, real bad situation. Even at our own school – I'm not telling you the details – it was just bad. But we got through it." As a team, the Lions were accustomed to the topic of race; though it was one they dealt with silently, without discussion.

At practice, Coach Bob Dwyer used it to motivate his players, making them believe the powers that be – "the people downtown" – did not believe that a team of blacks and whites could be that good.

"Dwyer used to always make reference to the people downtown thinking 'you all can't win, that you don't play together,' " Thompson said. "I don't know that we thought about it as much as it might be thought about today. That's the pitiful thing about it. You accepted your place and didn't think about it. ... Very seldom did anybody ever talk about racial issues.

"We were friends, all of us were friends. But they went their way socially and we went ours."

While many of his fellow starters graduated after the 1958-59 school year, Leftwich returned for his senior year. Leftwich regards the 1958-59 team as the best from his playing days, but the 1959-60 team posted a stunning 33-0 record.

The Lions handled Spingarn, 69-54, in the City Title Game. Then came the season's most dramatic moment, when Leftwich made a jumper to beat St. Catherine's of Racine, Wisconsin, in the Knights of Columbus championship at Georgetown.

"I threw the ball in and Walt Skinner got it," Barnes said. "I was scared Walt might take the shot. He caught it close to the sideline. Luckily, he dribbled and hit Leftwich at the top of the key."

When it came to picking a college, Leftwich had a tough choice. Father Duffy was married to the sister of St. Joe's Coach Jack Ramsay. Also recruiting Leftwich was Villanova, which was run by the Augustinians, who operated Carroll.

Leftwich chose Villanova, but his career was interrupted by a serious knee injury, sustained when he was driving with a friend to visit relatives in Bluefield, West Virginia. Just outside Charlottesville, Virginia, his friend fell asleep at the wheel and the car sideswiped an oil tanker. Leftwich was thrown from the car; he felt lucky to be alive.

"If it had hit head-on, it might have exploded," he said. "I feel very blessed."

Doctors wanted to perform exploratory surgery on his right knee, but Leftwich declined. Even though the injury would slow him a bit, he was not interested in an operation.

"They weren't paying one million bucks in those days" for pro basketball players, Leftwich said. "They were not paying enough for you to live the rest of your life off of. I figured what the heck, I could get a job and make close" to the same money.

"I could finish out being an average player and get on with my life. I'm happy with the life I've lived. If it happened today with one million on the table, they could cut me and figure out what the problem is."

Leftwich missed one season of basketball, then returned to the court before graduating in 1965. At Villanova, as at Carroll, he was a winner: In his three seasons at Villanova, the Wildcats went 21-7, 24-4 and 23-5.

Leftwich then returned to Washington, where he started to teach and coach at Carroll. He was the junior varsity coach for two years, then the varsity coach for six. He spent one year as an assistant coach to Thompson when he was hired at Georgetown, then was a salesman for Converse. After a foray into administration, he returned to the sidelines at Gwynn Park High, coaching the Yellow Jackets to two Maryland state titles before heading to the University of the District of Columbia, where he said he gathered enough material to write a book about the NCAA Division II school's follies.

"The problem was, was it fact or fiction?" Leftwich said. "The stories were fact, but they sounded like fiction. I was there for three years, but those were dog years so I have to multiply them by seven."

Leftwich continued his coaching career at Sidwell Friends School for thirteen years before returning to Carroll in 2005 as athletic director before retiring in 2013.

George married Mary in 1968 and they have two sons, George Jr. and Brian.

"It's been a fun run," he said. "Met some nice people. Sidwell is a different place. Met a lot of good people along the way. Three guys who played for me played pro ball: Eddie Jordan here [at Carroll]; Roger Mason, who started at Sidwell and finished at Good Counsel; and at Gwynn Park, Randolph Childress was a freshman my second year."

9. Len Bias

More than a quarter of a century after his death, the mention of Len Bias still evokes plenty of emotion -- from those who played or coached with or against him and those who merely watched his exploits on the basketball court.

Bias has been the subject of a book, *Lenny, Lefty and the Chancellor*.

Bias has been the subject of an award-winning documentary, *Without Bias*.

Newspapers and magazines occasionally look back to how Bias's death changed the basketball world – five years, ten years, twenty years, twenty-five later.

But while the highlight-reel plays for the University of Maryland still leave Internet viewers with their mouths agape, much less is known about Bias's formative years at Northwestern High School, just up the street from Cole Field House.

Some downplayed Bias's ability in high school. Others, though, insist that such thought is just talk.

"To tell you the truth, the only school he visited in the ACC was N.C. State and maybe he went to Oregon and that was it," said Lefty Driesell, who coached Maryland from 1969 to 1986. "A lot of people didn't recruit him much."

"Lefty always says he wasn't that highly recruited, but there were one hundred thirty schools that came in to talk to him," said Bob Wagner, who coached Bias at Northwestern. "I was a young coach and he was my first really big player. I gave everybody fifteen minutes. People got pissed off, but it was more about taking care of him. When he'd had enough, which he did, he would say, 'It all sounds the same to me right now.'"

Of course, it was easy to see why Driesell and others were interested in Bias.

Standing six-foot, seven-inches, he was long, lean and athletic. He could run the floor and was as competitive as anyone.

Twice cut during tryouts for the school team during his days at Greenbelt Junior High, Bias made the varsity as a sophomore at Northwestern. Wagner heard about the talented newcomer from some of his older players and quickly figured out ways to try to maximize his potential.

"Everybody knew the kid could play a little bit but he was out of control most of the time," Wagner said. "I guess that started my reputation of dealing with kids other coaches couldn't manage.

"After his tenth-grade year, he was constantly being developed. He worked hard. I think I had his trust. He knew whatever I did, whether he liked it or not, I was doing it for him.

"Leonard got interpreted as having a bad attitude, couldn't keep his mouth shut. But he wanted to win. He was a competitor. Guys like that should express themselves."

Because he was tall, Bias played in the post for the Wildcats. During practice and at other workouts, though, he drilled with the perimeter players in order to prepare for college.

Wagner also had a habit of never calling fouls on teammates defending Bias in practice; he wanted his star player to get used to contact so that in games he would not be bothered when opponents tried to play physical defense.

In games, Wagner signaled for a play called "five" nearly eighty percent of the time. It was not much of a play, though, simply designed for teammates to get the ball inside to Bias.

"Other teams knew that and they had to stop it," Wagner said.

Northwestern had not won much in the years after Harold Fox led the Hyattsville school to consecutive Maryland AA championships in 1967 and 1968. With Bias and some other talented players, though, the Wildcats rose toward the top.

During the 1980-81 season, as a junior, Bias scored twenty-three points as Northwestern beat the Eleanor Roosevelt Raiders, 101-61, to win its first Prince George's County title in more than a decade. Bias was named second-team All-Met after that season.

On the local television show "Fast Break," Bias told co-hosts Morgan Wootten and James Brown: "If you really do want to play basketball, you have to keep going out and work at it. Play as much as you can and take criticism. That's what I think I learned to do very well. I took criticism from everyone, people off the street. I took it and used it as a positive instead of a negative."

As a senior in 1981-82, Bias sat out the season's first two weeks. While there was speculation that the star player might transfer, Wagner was hoping to make a point. Bias was getting C's in two of his classes and teachers were telling the basketball coach that their student could be doing better.

"I didn't know it was going to happen, but that got him really focused," Wagner said. "He came back on the team and figured out where he wanted to go to school."

In an interesting twist, Bias wound up finishing his high school career on the floor of his future college team as Northwestern advanced to the Maryland AA championship game. But on a Saturday night at Cole Field House, the Wildcats suffered a dramatic loss. With one second left, Vernon Butler caught an inbounds pass and let fly a quick twenty-five footer that gave the High Point Eagles a 54-52 victory. Bias had eighteen points and thirteen rebounds and after the season was named first-team All-Met.

"He was gifted, but he worked very hard," Wagner said. "People don't give him enough credit for how hard he worked. He led every drill. He got most of the rebounds. All the effort things, the things people don't like doing."

As much as Bias improved through high school, Wootten said it was Bias's performance in the Capital Classic that cemented his place on the Washington-area basketball map. Bias scored eighteen points and grabbed eleven rebounds, sharing team most valuable player honors with Duke Blue Devils recruit Johnny Dawkins from Mackin as the Capital All-Stars beat the U.S. All-Stars, 82-79, before more than eleven thousand fans at Capital Centre.

"I did not know who he was until the Capital Classic," Wootten said. "He blossomed late in high school. We never played him, never scrimmaged him. Then, all of a sudden, wow! I'd heard about him when he was a senior, but I never met him until Adrian Branch introduced me to him at the University of Maryland. He was a late bloomer. That happens. Then everyone saw him at the Capital Classic and went gaga."

At Maryland, Bias saw his production rise each season. He averaged 7.2 points as a freshman, 15.3 points as a sophomore, 18.9 points as a junior and 23.2 points as a senior, earning first-team All-American honors. When the 1986 NBA Draft rolled around, Bias was the second overall selection, behind North Carolina forward Brad Daugherty.

Two days after the draft, early in the morning of June 19, 1986, after returning home from Boston following an introductory news conference where he signed a three million dollar endorsement contract with the shoe manufacturer Reebok, Bias died of a cocaine overdose while partying with some friends and teammates in his Washington Hall dormitory room.

It was a stunning turn of events. Here was a player regarded as one of the finest physical specimens falling unconscious and then dying after snorting cocaine with his friend, Brian Tribble.

At a memorial service in Cole Field House, Reverend Jesse L. Jackson told the audience that "God has called him to a higher purpose – to get the attention of this generation and save it."

Wayne K. Curry, the Bias family's attorney and future Prince George's County executive, years later told The Washington Post that Bias's death was "the most heartbreaking, stunning and paralyzing event. Nobody could grip the enormity of his spectacular rise and sudden demise."

Bias's death is among the most famous events in Washington basketball history, up there with DeMatha High beating Power Memorial and Lew Alcindor in 1965, the Kentucky versus Texas Western 1966 NCAA championship game at Cole Field House, the Bullets winning the 1978 NBA title, Georgetown winning the NCAA championship in 1984 and Maryland winning the 2002 NCAA championship.

In the months following Bias's death, change swept through the University of Maryland.

Athletic Director Dick Dull resigned in October. Three weeks later, Driesell – who once vowed to make Maryland the "UCLA of the East" and created Midnight Madness – was forced to followed suit. Task forces convened. Recommendations made. Changes followed. It became more of a challenge for coaches to recruit players to Maryland and get them admitted; one adopted recommendation was that coaches could not sign recruits to letters-of-intent without approval from the university admissions office.

Still, to this day, nearly everyone in the basketball community remembers where they were when learning of Bias's death and nearly all wonder about what might have been.

"It was just a shock," said the Hall of Fame former Georgetown coach John Thompson. "That had so much of an impact. I don't think it changed basketball as much as it made you so conscientious of his mistake and realize that a person can fall off a mountaintop. He was an inspiration to anybody who had to work hard. You saw the hard work that made him better and better. He was not a household name until he went to Maryland."

Make no mistake, though, just how big Bias had become by the time he completed his eligibility in College Park.

A few months after Bias died, Gary Williams left American University to become the coach at Ohio State. He had become familiar with Bias when he recruited one of his high school teammates, Darnell Swinton, to American, then followed Bias's career across town at his alma mater. (Williams is a 1968 Maryland graduate.) When he arrived at Ohio State, he wanted to get to know his new players and asked them to name the best player they faced the previous year.

"There were some great players in the Big Ten, but they all said Len Bias," said Williams, noting that Ohio State had beaten Maryland, 78-66, the previous year.

"I didn't see the game, but I saw the tape after I got the job [at Maryland] of the North Carolina game in the Dean Dome where he made a jump shot from the top of the circle, stole the inbounds pass and scored. I don't know how he got from the top of the circle to one step from the baseline.

"If he would have been in this era, I really feel he would have been LeBron James. He had those same skills. Back then, things were more regimented. ... Everybody knows what he was in college. It's nice to think he would have done the same thing in the NBA. The one thing he did was he kept getting better. I don't think he was at the peak of his game yet."

Said Wagner: "If he had lived, he had a great shot at creating a great rivalry, like [Larry] Bird and Magic [Johnson], but Jordan wins because Jordan lived. Leonard was a higher, stronger, better jumper than Jordan, but a different kind of player. There are a lot of guys in my lifetime better than Leonard, some might have been better than Jordan, but nobody will ever know because of drugs or they didn't live."

One of those players might have been Jay Bias, Len's younger brother who also was an All-Met basketball player at Northwestern, a player so talented that some thought he was better than his older brother. Lacking an SAT score high enough to qualify for a major-college scholarship, Jay Bias played for Allegany Junior College in Cumberland, Maryland, before returning home to pursue playing at a four-year school.

Before that could happen however, on December 5, 1990, tragedy again struck the Bias family again. Jay Bias, was shot and killed in the parking lot of a shopping mall following an argument with a stranger in a jewelry store.

8. Danny Ferry

The way Danny Ferry imagines it, he was just two or three days old, having returned from the hospital to his parents' home, when a basketball surely was placed in his crib.

With a father who played in the pros, then ran the local NBA franchise for seventeen years, it was only fitting that Danny – the youngest of three children – took to the hardwood like a natural.

Ever since, from DeMatha High to Duke University to a professional playing career and then a front-office job of his own in the NBA, the sport has been a prominent – dominant? – part of his life.

"It's been what has put food on our table, what my dad played and then worked at in the front office," Ferry said. "It's a big part of his identity and then our family's identity.

"It's important to note that it's a different time now, in that the scale of my dad's world was different then than it is now. Meaning, back then, there were seven or eight people in an NBA office. Now there are three hundred. It was so much more intimate than it is now. The people that worked for the team and played on the team, at some level, were a part of our family."

And in the Ferry family, basketball was a big deal.

Bob Ferry starred at Saint Louis University, then played ten seasons in the NBA, the final five with the Baltimore Bullets. After his playing career, he became the team's assistant coach and then the general manager, building the Washington Bullets squad that won the 1978 league championship.

Bob and Rita's first child, Lucy, was not inclined to play basketball. But her two younger brothers were. In fact, just two years apart in age, Bobby and Danny were so competitive that their one-on-one games on the court at home rarely finished before a fight developed as they argued about a call.

While Bobby topped out at six-foot, four-inches, Danny continued to sprout. In the few months after his eighth-grade season at Saint Mark's and before starting basketball season the following fall at DeMatha, Danny grew a staggering six inches. He was now six-nine.

A senior on the DeMatha varsity, Bobby was going to have the share time with his freshman brother.

The Stags were a basketball powerhouse. DeMatha regularly won the Washington-area Catholic league championship, finished atop The Washington Post's rankings and competed for the top spot in national rankings.

Being on the varsity as a freshman might be difficult for some to handle – Coach Morgan Wootten almost never kept ninth-graders on the team – but Ferry was used to the spotlight. After all, how many kids could annually guarantee their youth-league team would get to play full court before several thousand folks at the Capital Centre as halftime entertainment? And Ferry was used to being around older, taller, seasoned opponents: At every opportunity, Bob would take his boys to practice or games. They could watch top players, and occasionally would get on the court during workouts and either rebound or take some shots themselves.

"The exposure that I was afforded at a young age, from being around NBA players and having a dad who could teach you how to shoot, put a basketball hoop on an asphalt pad with a light on it so you could shoot at night – it was a part of your life," Ferry said. "It's just what we did.

"You go to so many games. I'd go to a lot of University of Maryland games with my dad when he was scouting as well. I have a picture of me sitting on his lap when I was six years old at Cole Field House. You're just around it so much.

"One of my strengths was probably from that – I can think on the court and see things from an abstract way. It helped me with passing, it helped me with shots that athletically I wasn't going to be able to create on my own."

Bob Ferry did not insist that his boys hone their game on the basketball court. But seeing that they enjoyed the sport, he wanted to position his sons to succeed. If that meant joining a team at a District boys' club to play against better opposition – where the Ferrys were the only white boys – so be it. Eventually, Bobby and Danny learned to ride the Metro train from New Carrollton so that their parents did not have to drive them and wait for a practice or game to end.

"Taking the subway down, my parents didn't think anything of it," Danny said with a laugh. "I don't think a lot of parents would do that now."

"People probably thought he had an advantage because I was in the business. But mostly the advantage I had was I knew enough to send him to good coaches and put him in competitive situations," Bob Ferry said.

Having an older brother who knew the ropes helped. Bobby chose DeMatha over St. John's, Bowie and Eleanor Roosevelt. Danny would follow in his footsteps.

By the time Danny enrolled at DeMatha as a fourteen-year-old freshman, he had grown accustomed to the environment at the all-boys' school just off U.S. 1 in Hyattsville. During the seventh and eighth grades at Saint Mark's, Danny often would get a ride over to DeMatha to watch, and sometimes participate in, pickup games before riding home with Bobby. Danny also would tag along – and hope to get in the game – when Bobby went to play pickup over at Cole Field House with the University of Maryland players.

Danny also was familiar with the legendary Wootten. Every summer, he would attend the Metropolitan Area Basketball School run by Wootten and St. John's Coach Joe Gallagher.

"I started going there as young as you could, I think eight or nine years old," Ferry said. "Did it for two weeks every summer. When you were at DeMatha, of course, you worked the camp. You didn't make much, but those were great times. I look back at going to the Metropolitan Basketball School and it was great. Those are the first times you're getting out of your world. Growing up in Bowie, you played for the boys' club but didn't know the other kids and the scope of the teams you played was very small.

"Going to MABS, you got to play against kids from Virginia, from the District, from Maryland. There was a melting pot of diversity and talent. And they made it fun."

Although Ferry had plenty of talent, Wootten wanted to simplify his transition to the high school game. Wootten told Ferry that, as the first player off the bench, he should not to worry about scoring, to focus only on rebounding. Ferry averaged seven points and four rebounds that season, then joined the starting lineup as a sophomore and averaged 10.4 points and seven rebounds. The next season, Ferry improved to 16.3 points and seven rebounds per game. His clutch free throws in the final seconds lifted the Stags to a 76-73 victory over the Dunbar Poets, ending the Baltimore school's fifty-nine-game winning streak.

At the end of that 1983-84 season, DeMatha was ranked first nationally and Dunbar was second. Ferry was named All-Met and the recruiting chase was on. Except for one thing: With a veteran coach accustomed to the recruiting furor and a father in the business, things did not get crazy for Ferry.

"I didn't have a lot of people that were influencers in my life," Ferry said. "In some ways, I was kind of in a little bit of a bubble. I walked into it thinking I wanted to go away for school, but I wanted to play in the ACC because I had gone to Maryland games from a young age and seen those games. The Big East was just making it at that time. John Thompson had his first big success when I was in high school. ...

"Outside the ACC, I really only talked to three schools at all: Kentucky, Kansas and Notre Dame. I kind of grew up a Carolina fan. Had I signed early, I probably would have signed at Carolina. But I hadn't felt it in my gut yet."

Maryland Coach Lefty Driesell, of course, took the hint that Ferry wanted to go away for college. When Ferry made his official visit to campus, Driesell had Ferry driven from DeMatha to the College Park airport, where he boarded a small private plane and flew over Cole Field House, where a sign "Danny's House" was perched on the green arched roof. For Ferry's trip to Virginia, Cavaliers Coach Terry Holland sent a limousine to take Ferry from DeMatha to the College Park airport, where a helicopter flew him to Charlottesville.

"If I don't have to [fly in a helicopter] again, that's okay," Ferry said. "But back then I was bright-eyed and bushy-tailed. It was a cool experience, that's for sure."

Duke and North Carolina were a bit more subtle. What might have put the Blue Devils over the top, however, was having a coach at every DeMatha game that season.

"Coach K probably came to ten of my high school games in the middle of his season," Ferry said of Mike Krzyzewski, the legendary Duke coach. "If he wasn't there, Bob Bender or Chuck Swenson was at my game. I remember that. I didn't talk to them, but I knew they were there."

Why were so many coaches in such hot pursuit?

Ferry had grown to six-ten, but he still had the ability to play on the perimeter. He could post up or shoot a jump shot. And, after all those years playing against his brother and other older players, Ferry knew how to play the game.

"What's that old John Wooden statement -- you better learn the trade before you learn the tricks of the trade?" Wootten said. "Well, Danny knew both."

"He was so far advanced in the tricks of the trade and he was so fundamentally sound – he was way older than the kids he was playing against in high school," said Pete Strickland, who was an assistant coach at DeMatha during Ferry's senior year and now is an assistant at George Washington University. "And also very skilled for his size, which was unusual. He was a classic carpenter's son in the carpenter's game. He knew everything about the game. He was [Larry] Birdish. He was two plays ahead of people. He got bored at times."

That senior year, Ferry averaged twenty points, 15.7 rebounds, three assists and three blocks. He repeated as an All-Met and was selected national Player of the Year by Parade magazine and USA Today. (Spingarn guard Sherman Douglas, after leading the Green Wave to a City Title Game victory over DeMatha, was The Post's Player of the Year.)

Two days after playing in the Capital Classic, Ferry committed to play for Duke.

At Duke, Ferry helped the Blue Devils reach the Final Four three times in four years – though he nearly was not a part of that last trip. After his junior year, Ferry decided to enter the NBA draft. He expected to be drafted anywhere from seventh to tenth overall – but Krzyzewski persuaded him to stay at Duke.

"Which was some of the best advice someone had ever given me," Ferry said. "That senior year was so fulfilling and so enjoyable. I remember being in my bedroom and calling him and letting him know, and I think it caught him a little off guard. We talked and talked a couple times after that. I ended up getting insurance from Lloyd's of London. That made me feel a little more at ease."

Ferry was one of the final cuts from the 1988 U.S. Olympic team, sidelined by a knee injury that prevented him from participating in training camp. He recovered well enough that early that senior season, he scored fifty-eight points (making twenty-three of twenty-six shots) in a 117-102 victory over Miami (Fla.), which still stands as the ACC single-game scoring record. He repeated as ACC Player of the Year and was named the national Player of the Year.

By staying for his senior season, Ferry had vaulted toward the top of the NBA draft. But when the Los Angeles Clippers took him with the second overall pick, Ferry was less than thrilled. A woeful franchise, the Clippers had drafted forwards Danny Manning and Ken Norman the previous year, and Ferry felt it was a less than perfect fit. He had been hoping to go to the San Antonio Spurs at the third pick, having spent plenty of time training during summers in Annapolis with soon-to-be Spurs rookie David Robinson, who had starred at the Naval Academy.

That draft night, having left Madison Square Garden and walking back to his hotel, Ferry was approached by a stranger, who introduced himself as the coach of an Italian team. Would Ferry be interested in playing the 1989-90 season for Il Messagero instead of going to the Clippers?

"Here's my number -- you can call me," Ferry said. He did not take Valerio Bianchini seriously at all and thought he would never hear from the man again, but for some reason he gave Bianchini his phone number. "I don't know what I'll do."

Sure enough, the phone rang the next day. And Bianchini and his operatives kept calling.

Ferry was planning to visit a college roommate in Italy anyway, so he figured there was nothing to be lost in taking up the offer to visit Rome. Instead of flying coach on United Airlines, Ferry and a friend, Lou Sherr, flew over on the Concorde.

"Lou won," Ferry said.

After Ferry was wined and dined, team owner Raul Gardini made a contract offer for five years, with an out to go to the NBA after each season. It wasn't the NBA, but it wasn't bad.

In subsequent negotiations, trying to stall for time and hopeful the Clippers would make a trade, Ferry's agent, David Falk, presented Gardini with a list of demands. He wanted a secretary, cooks, security, Italian lessons. But instead of getting a counterproposal, Falk was told that all would be fine. So would a few extra plane tickets for family to visit.

Ferry played one year for Il Messagero, and the Clippers traded his rights to the Cleveland Cavaliers. Ferry signed with the Cavs and had a solid if not spectacular pro career. Over ten seasons in Cleveland and three in San Antonio, he averaged seven points and 2.8 rebounds.

Upon finishing his playing career in 2003, Ferry went into the front office. After two seasons working for the Spurs, he was hired as the Cavaliers' general manager. He spent five years in that capacity before leaving after the 2009-10 season and returning to San Antonio as vice president of basketball operations. He was named President of Basketball Operations and General Manager of the Atlanta Hawks from 2012 to 2015.

Danny and his wife, Tiffany, have five children: Hannah, Grace, Sophia, Lucy and Jackson.

7. Wil Jones

Everybody, it seems, has a story about Wil Jones. Most of them are true, though a few appear to be legends that have grown over the years since he started ruling local basketball courts in the 1950s.

Yes, the five-foot, ten-inch Jones would tell you how he was going to beat you. Then he did it. Then he told you how he did it. And how he was going to do it again.

"Wil Jones was the Muhammad Ali of the basketball court," said John Thompson, who was a few years younger than Jones as the two grew up playing basketball in the city before eventually becoming college basketball coaches. "Everyone would say, 'There's that little m----------,' or whatever. But everybody respected him because he was very good."

One day over at the Number Two Metropolitan Police Boys Club, Jones was fouled and got hit in the eye. Some of those watching from the sideline started to harass him.

"I don't need but one eye," he said before making both free throws.

Morgan Wootten, before he began coaching at DeMatha Catholic High, was officiating a game during Jones's senior year at Dunbar High in 1956. A foul was called late in the game, with Dunbar trailing by a point.

"Give me this ball and let me get it even," Jones said as he stepped to the free throw line.

After making the first shot, Jones had plenty of confidence for the second try -- not that he ever lacked in that department. "Now let's get the right team ahead here," Jones said as Wootten bounced the ball to him.

"He was something," Wootten said.

Who else has a scar on the back of his head from when a cousin bit him during a supposed friendly game at Turkey Thicket playground?

"I faked him, and he bit me in the head because I was kicking his ass," Jones said. "They had to take me to the emergency room."

If there were a mayor of Washington-area basketball, Wil Jones would be the king.

Who else says he gave Adrian Dantley his first basketball?

Who else got George Leftwich into a regular game with older players over at the Park View playground?

Who else did Oscar Robertson think of when learning that a visitor to Cincinnati was from Washington?

"One of the first things he said to me when he found out was, 'How's that bigmouth Willie Jones?'" Thompson said.

Who else thought he was the best player ever from the city, as he spent half the year in Virginia Beach in retirement while battling cancer.

"If you talk to him and Wil is not your Number One, Wil is going to get on you," Sherman Douglas, the former Spingarn point guard, said. "Wil talks, 'I can kick your butt now.' And he's old! If confidence gets you Number One, he's probably Number One."

"Today, he thinks he can still compete," Gary Williams said a few years ago, noting that Jones was still the all-time leading scorer at American University when Williams was hired to coach there in 1978. Jones has since fallen to third on that list, with 1,982 points in three seasons, though he still holds the school's single-game scoring record of fifty-four points in a game, set in an NCAA Division II tournament game against Evansville University.

Yes, up until he died on March 12, 2015, Wil Jones still had it. Who else, despite a bad back that has limited his ability to walk up the stairs in his house, would get so fired up mid-sentence, waving his finger in your face to prove his point?

"If I played four years, I'd have scored one million points! We didn't have a three-point line. Remember that! I might have scored six thousand in college if I'd had that!" Jones said, just getting started.

"I told the truth. It's different talking and telling the truth. I tell you, 'F--- with me and I'll give you thirty. Leave me alone, I'll take eighteen and we'll take our normal win. Overf--- with me and I'll give you fifty!' I told the truth in my mind. I bragged and was cocky in your mind, until I did it. Then that little black son of a bitch walked away!

"That's why they liked me, because I didn't lie. Suppose I said all that s--- and then didn't deliver? I was serious about one thing: When I stepped in the lines to play basketball, I didn't want anyone to beat me. Because I saw this day coming and didn't want anybody to be able to say he kicked my ass!"

Nobody got the best of Wil Jones, who was a fighter, basically, since he was born on March 3, 1938, the second son of Lottie and Frank Jones.

"My momma looked like you and my daddy looked this telephone," he said, picking up a black handset. "I was on the third floor at Columbia Hospital and the only thing that messed me up was my daddy. They didn't let black people on the third floor. They moved my ass so fast [to the second floor] where they didn't have windows. It stunted my growth!"

Frank Jones was a waiter on the Pennsylvania Railroad. Lottie was a housewife, often taking into the family's Lamont Road Northwest home men who came from the South to do construction and women who came to do domestic work

William, or Willie, as he soon came to be known, looked up to his older brother, Frank, but in their formative years Frank wanted nothing to do with a sibling two years younger. It was Willie's close friend, O'Donnell Hooks, who taught him how to play basketball.

"He taught everybody that played basketball in Northwest Washington," Jones said. "He was twelve years old and he could play!"

Hooks went to Cardozo High, where Jones was supposed to attend. "But I didn't want to play with O'Donnell," Jones said. "All the girls liked him. He was too good. I wanted to get in the game and get a girl, too!"

So Jones went to Dunbar, which "was the school for the tenderoni, the sissified, the elite," he said. "You couldn't be an athlete there. You had to go to Phelps or Armstrong or Cardozo."

Jones played on the junior varsity as a sophomore during the 1953-54 school year, then joined the varsity the next season, averaging nearly fifteen points per game. As a senior in 1955-56, Jones tore it up, scoring forty-five points in an early-season rout of Western High and forty in a victory over Theodore Roosevelt. Jones led the Crimson Tide to the Interhigh championship game, in which he scored twenty-nine points, but Dunbar lost to Armstrong, 72-58. Jones was named first-team All-Metropolitan.

Jones wanted to play for Michigan State, familiar with the Spartans from seeing them on television. "But they told me I was too small and would only give me a partial scholarship," he said.

Willie Wood, the former Armstrong star who eventually was enshrined in the Pro Football Hall of Fame after a long career with the Green Bay Packers, wanted Jones to go with him to Coalinga Junior College in central

California, "but they told me I was too small, too," Jones said. "I'm still pissed off, because I sent them my scrapbook and they never sent it back!"

Jones said he could have played baseball in the Pittsburgh Pirates organization but preferred to play basketball.

"I pitched and played center field, but I could bat," Jones said. "But I wanted the girls, the hoorah. The instant hoorah. I loved the sound of the crowd. You weren't getting that s--- in the minor leagues."

In the fall of 1956, though, with Jones having graduated from Dunbar a few months earlier but having re-enrolled to take a second foreign language (Latin) to get ready for college, one day Dunbar Coach Snake Williams took him to American University to meet the basketball coach and athletic director, Dave Carrasco. Williams asked Carrasco if he wanted to watch Jones play; but Carrasco simply wanted Jones to sign scholarship papers.

Jones balked, but that night Carrasco and his coaches came to Lamont Street and made a pitch to Frank Jones.

"The only thing he heard was they wanted to offer Wil a four-year scholarship for his education and it will be free if we can get Wil to sign this paper," Jones said.

That was it: Jones was bound for American University. He enrolled for the spring semester and made his debut on the basketball court for the 1957-58 school year, leading the Eagles to three consecutive NCAA Division II tournament berths.

As a sophomore, Jones scored thirty points in a 94-67 victory over Georgetown, the Eagles' first victory in seventeen games between the schools. Newspaper accounts called it American's finest athletic moment.

Jones was named an honorable mention all-American as a junior in 1959 and followed that by being named an NCAA College Division all-American as a senior in 1960. He averaged twenty-five points as a junior and 23.9 as a senior. In his final collegiate game, Jones made eighteen of forty-one shots and eighteen of twenty-two free throws to tally fifty-four points in a 101-91 loss to Evansville.

He earned an invitation to the 1960 (and 1964) Olympic tryouts where, surprise, he again was told he was too short.

Selected in the twelfth round of the NBA draft by the Minneapolis Lakers, Jones – despite at one point saying he was now 5-11¾, again was told he was too short. He played two years in the American Basketball League before going into teaching and coaching. He started as an elementary school physical education teacher in Alexandria and worked as an assistant basketball coach at Wakefield High in Arlington.

Then Fairfax County opened Robinson Secondary School in Fairfax, and Jones was hired as the school's first basketball coach – the only black high school basketball coach at the time in Northern Virginia.

Jones said the other high school coaches didn't approve of a black coach being selected. "So they said, 'Let's take Wil, we'll fire this black m----------- in a year!'" Jones said. "They made a mistake. I went out there and turned all those white boys into winners."

In five seasons at Robinson, Jones had a record of 76-19. Then Dave Pritchett left Maryland's coaching staff and the remaining assistant, Joe Harrington, suggested Jones apply for the opening. Jones was interested but, naturally, wanted Coach Lefty Driesell to make the first move.

At his job interview, Driesell asked Jones if he could recruit.

"I'm from Washington! I can recruit Washington better than you!" Jones retorted.

Jones spent the next four seasons on Maryland's staff before leaving to become the head coach at the University of the District of Columbia. Just like when he played, Jones talked a big game, saying that he was going to challenge Georgetown and Howard and play for a national title within five years. Even though he couldn't get on the floor to back things up, Jones succeeded. He lured the talented Earl Jones from Spingarn High and won the NCAA Division II title in 1983.

"Just like saying, 'I'm going to make this jump shot on you left-handed,'" Jones said. "You got it? That's why they had trouble with me."

To celebrate, Jones went out and bought a Cadillac.

"Because my father never bought a car," he said. "But he said if he could buy one, he would buy one that would go from Lamont Street to the Monument and back without the motor getting hot. I asked what kind of car was that, and he said a Cadillac."

In 1999, Jones moved up to the NCAA Division I level when he was hired at Norfolk State. Jones lasted three seasons there, compiling a 34-52 record. He was fired after the 2001-02 season but remained as enthusiastic as ever when he gets talking about basketball.

"That started when I was in high school. That's before Muhammad Ali," Jones said. "I started talking in high school. I was boosting myself up. A lot of people think you are self-serving and cocky, but I was trying to keep myself at a level where I could be good. I don't think size has s--- to do with a person being good."

6. Jack George

He threw the football well enough to earn a scholarship to play quarterback for the University of Notre Dame.

He earned All-American honors on the basketball court at La Salle University and went on to play eight seasons in the National Basketball Association.

And he was talented enough on the baseball diamond, drafted by the old Philadelphia A's, and nearly making it to the majors.

Was there anything Jack George couldn't do?

His longtime friend, the legendary Mount St. Mary's basketball coach Jim Phelan, joked that George could do anything but hit a golf ball.

"He couldn't get it," Phelan said. "Here was a ball that never moved until you hit it."

Everything else, though, the affable George could handle.

A 1948 graduate of St. John's College High School – back when the private school's campus was located downtown on Vermont Avenue, before it moved to its current location on Military Road next to Rock Creek Park -- George also was an elite junior tennis player.

As an adult, he excelled on the softball field and was inducted into the Washington D.C. Metro Fastpitch Hall of Fame.

"The second-best basketball player that came out of this area was Jack George," said longtime St. John's basketball coach Joe Gallagher. "Not because he was my player. The best was Elgin Baylor. But Jack was probably the best all-around athlete that's come out of Washington."

The six-foot, two-inch George also was a very good boxer, according to Phelan, who was his basketball teammate for one year at La Salle and again in the NBA with the Philadelphia Warriors.

"He had five knockouts one night in Wildwood," Phelan, who was two years ahead of George at La Salle, recalled of one trip to the Jersey Shore that must have been memorable. "He got the bouncer at the Riptide twice."

George's athletic prowess started before high school. It carried over to his sophomore year at McKinley Tech and then to two years at St. John's.

Those were low-scoring days on the basketball court, but George put up big numbers. As a junior, he scored half of the Cadets' points, fourteen, in a 28-26 victory over La Salle of Cumberland. George netted twenty-two in a 46-36 victory at Anacostia and twenty-two in a 54-34 victory over Theodore Roosevelt. When St. John's avenged an earlier loss to Coolidge, George scored fifteen points in a 29-25 victory.

At season's end, having averaged seventeen points per game and led St. John's to second place in the All-Metropolitan Tournament, George was selected to The Washington Post's All-Metro team:

Jack George, the only junior on the first team, 'made' the St. John's club that won the Catholic High title, and was runner up to Coolidge in the metropolitan tournament.

In the spring, George played outfield and third base on the baseball team, batting .367 and attracting yet more attention. St. John's baseball coach Gene Augusterfer spoke to scouts from the Chicago Cubs and Boston Red Sox who were interested in signing George to a pro contract after he graduated from St. John's the next year, The Post reported.

The exploits continued on the football field the following fall.

George was tough, excelling at quarterback and defensive back. He could run or pass. He was a ballhawk at defensive back. He also kicked extra points and punted.

Gallagher, who also coached football for a few years, remembered a 36-20 victory over Blair in which holding and illegal procedure penalties negated consecutive touchdown passes by George. It was not a problem, though, as the coach hollered for George to run the same play yet again.

"He threw the third touchdown pass and everything was okay," Gallagher said, noting that George finished the game with four touchdown passes that counted.

In the season's biggest showdown, before more than ten thousand fans at Griffith Stadium, George threw three touchdown passes – two to Tom Fannon – in a 19-0 victory over Central High. By beating the Vikings, who were tied for the lead in the Interhigh public school league, the Cadets staked their claim to an unofficial city championship.

Four weeks later, George capped the Cadets' 9-0 season with a one-yard quarterback sneak for a touchdown with fifty-five seconds left for a 12-6 victory over rival Gonzaga. Again, ten thousand spectators were at Griffith Stadium for the game.

Not surprisingly, George was named The Post's Player of the Year after completing more than sixty percent of his passes, throwing an area-best eighteen touchdown passes and leading the Cadets to their first-ever undefeated season. An article accompanying the selection described George as "St. John's one-man riot squad."

George's final season of high school basketball was simply more of the same for a teenager who had grown accustomed to dominating the competition. George kept scoring points and St. John's won a lot of games, including a 38-33 victory over Gonzaga in the Catholic league championship as he scored a game-high seventeen points. He then scored a tournament record thirty-one points in a 53-51 victory over Central in the final of the All-Metropolitan Tournament at the University of Maryland's Ritchie Coliseum.

Just like football season, George was named The Post's Player of the Year:

Master of every type of shot, George compiled a 15-point per game average. The versatile 6 foot 1 inch star was also an excellent ball handler, and set up many scoring plays for his teammates. His coach, Joe Gallagher, said of George, "He was the difference between St. John's being a championship team and just another good team."

George had no problems on the football field, basketball court or baseball diamond.

Mastering the art of picking a college, however, was quite different, as schools in the region and across the country made their pitches.

Then there was the decision of which sport to pursue.

He "definitely agreed" to enroll in five different colleges, The Post reported.

Finally, though, on May 25, 1948, George made his choice. He would play football at Notre Dame. The Fighting Irish were coming off consecutive national championships under Coach Frank Leahy, winning seventeen of eighteen games over those two seasons, the lone blemish a 0-0 tie against Army in 1946 that was regarded as the "Game of the Century." In 1947, Notre Dame quarterback Johnny Lujack won the Heisman Trophy.

George, though, never had a chance at the Heisman. By the time the Fighting Irish won their next national title in 1949 – when George would have been a sophomore – he was back on the East Coast, having traded in his cleats for a pair of high-tops.

After one year as a backup quarterback on the freshman team, George left South Bend, telling The Post that the school was too far from home and "failed to live up to certain promises."

"He went to school to play football at Notre Dame, but they wouldn't let him play basketball," McKinley Tech standout Stan "Snookie" Kernan said. "That's why he went to La Salle."

Not only did George switch schools, he switched sports; La Salle had disbanded its football team after the 1941 season because of declining male enrollment due to World War II.

After not playing a sport during the 1949-50 school year to become eligible at La Salle, George burst onto the scene the next year, earning the President's Cup given by university administrators to the school's top athlete. He scored a school-record 469 points during the basketball season and batted .449 with twenty-two runs batted in while playing catcher during baseball season.

"He was such a fantastic athlete," Phelan said. "He finished up well in a national sixteen-and-under tennis tournament and beat [future professional star] Tony Trabert. I remember one year we played Cincinnati in Cincinnati Gardens and Tony Trabert was on the bench on the basketball team. Jack said, 'I'm going to kick his ass here, too.' He was a tough competitor."

But with two years of athletic eligibility remaining, George was drafted into the Army. Stationed at Fort Belvoir in Northern Virginia, George played on the base's basketball and baseball teams. There he ran back into Phelan, who was in the Marine Corps and was based at nearby Quantico.

"Jack was the toughest guy on that team, too," Phelan said. "They won the all-Army, we won the all-Marines. But he had to miss the all-service tournament because he was getting married."

After two years in the Army, George was discharged. Now he moved on to pro sports.

Selected in the 1953 NBA draft by the Philadelphia Warriors, George enjoyed an eight-year career. He played in the 1956 and 1957 NBA All-Star games and was annually among the league's assist leaders. He also remained a tough customer, said Phelan, who was teammates with him for one season in Philadelphia.

During one game at the Boston Garden, teammate Neil Johnston got tangled up with Celtics star Bob Cousy at the scorer's table. Things started getting ugly when Johnston slung Cousy into the scorer's table, prompting several players to come charging off the Celtics' bench.

"Should we go up there?" Phelan asked George, not necessarily in a hurry to get involved in the brouhaha.

"[Screw] him, I don't really like him anyway," George replied, also content to remain in what had become a ringside seat.

However, moments later, Celtics center Bob Brannum, who fancied himself as Cousy's personal protector, started lumbering toward the mass of players. That's when George decided to intercept the six-five reserve.

"Let's go," George told Phelan. "I want a part of this guy!"

Phelan shook his head and told George, "You're nuts!" before going along.

"Where the heck are you going?" George growled at Brannum. "Go back to the bench before I pound you into next week!"

Brannum didn't like it, but he soon relented.

George spent 5½ seasons with the Warriors and 2 ½ seasons with the New York Knicks. He spent a few offseasons playing minor league baseball but struggled to hit curveballs, Phelan said. After retiring, George worked first for a moving company in Philadelphia and then for an office-machine company in Chicago.

"How's the house that Jack built?" George would ask Gallagher when phoning to check in on his former coach.

One time, when visiting his mother, George got a call from Gallagher. His former coach was seeking an afternoon tennis partner for Celtics Coach Red Auerbach, who lived just a few blocks from St. John's and was speaking at Gallagher's summer camp the next morning.

Auerbach had easily dispatched of the first player arranged by Gallagher and asked for a more challenging match.

It had been a few years since George last picked up a racket, but that was no obstacle when he learned the opponent's identity, as he and Auerbach had had an adversial relationship from George's NBA days.

"I've got some shoes," George told Gallagher. "I'll be there."

That led Gallagher to call Auerbach.

"I've got a match for you, and he's younger than you are and I think he's better than you are," Gallagher said.

"Who is it?" Auerbach replied.

"Jack George."

"I'll be there," Auerbach said.

It was not much of a match, George reported to Gallagher. The final score was 6-0, 6-0.

"Red didn't come in the office that day," Gallagher said. "He hopped in his Mercedes and went right home."

Jack George, it seemed, could play nearly anything.

George and Lois had two sons, Gary and Jack, before she died.

George later moved to North Fort Myers, Florida, and was engaged to Pat Zimmerman when he died of cancer on January 30, 1989.

5. Grant Hill

Growing up in Reston, Virginia, about thirty minutes west of downtown Washington, Grant Hill was keenly aware of stereotypes and other people's perceptions.

The best basketball supposedly was found in the inner city, where the players were tougher and more streetwise than their counterparts from the suburbs.

As the son of Calvin Hill, who spent twelve years as a running back in the National Football League and was a four-time Pro Bowl selection, Hill supposedly somehow had it easier than a normal teenager.

"There was always a feeling that I had to prove myself," Hill said. "People automatically thought, 'Okay, you're privileged, you don't have that hunger.' ... Not really having the suburban game – a guy going to the hole and dunking on people, it was a way to prove whatever perceptions, beliefs, stereotypes people had. I wanted to try to change that."

Being from Reston had its advantages, though.

Hill could look across the community and see a slightly older player from South Lakes High School – Michael Jackson, who had gone on to play at Georgetown University and then in the NBA. He could look a few miles away and see Dennis Scott, three years older than Hill, go on to play at Georgia Tech, where he was named the 1989-90 Atlantic Coast Conference Player of the Year before heading to the NBA. Other players also recently had made it from Northern Virginia to high levels of basketball, such as Tommy Amaker (a 1983 W.T. Woodson High graduate) and Billy King (a 1984 Park View High graduate), both of whom starred at Duke University.

"I used to see their AAU games, their high school games, the Capital Classic games," Hill said. "High school basketball, I was into as much as, if not more than, college basketball. ... I would go to games on Friday nights, almost idolizing these guys."

A few years later, other youngsters were idolizing Grant Hill.

He will go down as one of the finest players ever from the Washington area, having starred at South Lakes, then at Duke and then in the NBA, where he played eighteen seasons and was selected an all-star seven times.

Hill twice led South Lakes to the Virginia High School League's Group AAA tournament semifinals. He helped Duke win NCAA championships in his first two years of college, then as a senior led the Blue Devils to a third title game appearance. His professional career got off to a roaring start, then was derailed by ankle surgeries in three consecutive seasons before a remarkable comeback.

His experiences, though, all started as a tot who tagged along with his father to football sidelines and locker rooms.

"Especially when my dad was in Cleveland" from 1978 to 1981, Hill said. "Having the access with these athletes, I guess, is a dream for every kid who is a sports fan. I'm not a huge football fan now, but I remember the late '70s – Redskins Park, I was over there all the time, even after my dad left. When I was in college and had a problem, I'd go over there and the trainers would work on me. It was kind of neat to grow up like that and be around it.

"I don't think my dad ever thought I'd be a professional athlete, but the various values you learn from sports, you apply that to life. Teach your son lessons. I don't think he was trying to be like the late Earl Woods [father of Tiger Woods] and turn me into a professional athlete, but maybe indirectly he was. It just happened that way."

It was a two-way street. Calvin Hill enjoyed having his son around.

"My dad was fortunate because he was older and he had a kid," Grant Hill said. "Most of the guys didn't have kids who were seven, eight or nine years old who could tag along and go into the locker room and when an ex-teammate came to town could go out to dinner. I could tag along. That's kind of all I knew, growing up in professional sports."

Grant also enjoyed playing sports. But he was not allowed to play football at an early age.

Calvin and Janet Hill wanted their only child to play other sports and then maybe, if he wanted, he could play football later on. At first, Grant excelled at soccer.

"I'm left-footed, I played left wing," he said. "I was actually on a pretty good team, a travel team that won the state championship. A lot of the guys went on to play in college. … At that point, I was probably more into soccer than I was basketball."

"He was about the tallest soccer player out there and also had a bush to go with it," said Galvin Morris, a high school classmate of Hill's who coached baseball at his alma mater for 15 seasons.

However, as he got older – and taller – Hill took a liking to basketball. A year before entering high school, Hill's AAU team won the national tournament.

"That was when it just all of a sudden clicked: I'm playing against the best my age," he said. "The shift from soccer to basketball happened overnight. I never played soccer again."

So much for the idea of playing for the South Lakes soccer team. Hill, though, still wanted to play basketball on the school's freshman team with his classmates.

Seahawks basketball coach Wendell Byrd had other thoughts. He knew that Hill would be on the varsity as a freshman. When the Seahawks' players had pickup games during after-school open gyms, Byrd made sure his newcomer took part in the action.

"He was playing on a side court and Coach Byrd would be there and say, 'No, you're on the center court,'" said Darryl Branch, a guard who was one year ahead of Hill.

"I played and started," Hill said. "From that point on, there was no more soccer."

Hill never wanted the spotlight, but he could not avoid it, either.

He would stand to the side of the open gyms, tryouts and early-season practices. It was as if, somehow, not being front and center might make him invisible. He was comfortable around the older players, but did not want to intrude on their world.

Some of those older players were plenty curious about the tall newcomer in their midst, including Herb Williams-Baffoe, who as a senior expected to start for the first time when Hill was a freshman in the 1986-87 season.

"I'm sticking my chest out, like, 'Okay, this guy is coming to take my spot and that's not cool with me,'" Williams-Baffoe said. "They get out on the court and I'm like, 'Okay, I'm guarding him,' trying to show off to the coaches."

Hill got the ball and tried to drive baseline.

Williams-Baffoe was not about to let that happen.

"I gave him a little hip check and he landed on his behind," Williams-Baffoe said. "And I'm thinking, 'This guy is not so tough.' The coaches were sitting around talking -- they weren't so concerned. It wasn't a malicious hit like I came over his shoulder. I gave him a little hip check, let him know he was coming to play with the big boys."

Hill never complained. Soon enough, the older players got used to their younger teammate. Hill averaged ten points and eight rebounds starting at power forward as a freshman. He and point guard John Lewis scored sixteen points apiece in a 67-63 victory over Madison in the Great Falls District tournament semifinals. In the district final against Washington-Lee, Hill dunked an alley-oop pass in the closing seconds of a 61-57 victory, a play that his former teammates still remember. South Lakes was not yet a power – the Seahawks were barely over .500 that season – but the seeds were planted for Hill to be a very good player.

But while Hill blended in on the court, he rarely ventured out with his teammates.

Though he lived just behind South Lakes and could walk to school in less than 10 minutes, Hill often got a ride to school in the morning from Lewis, who lived down the street.

"Man, you're on the varsity, you can't walk to school," Lewis would say jokingly.

Lewis also would drive Hill home after practice or games. After dropping Hill off after a Friday night game, however, Lewis was likely to head back out and meet his teammates. Hill never would ask Lewis where he was going.

"It was like pulling teeth to get him to go out – he would never, ever," Williams-Baffoe said. "Everybody was treating us like kings [at parties] and he probably had scored twenty-five points that night."

"I think those guys probably recognized my talents and abilities more so than I did," Hill said. "I didn't hang out with them. I was fourteen years old. I wasn't doing what they were doing. I was still socially with kids my own age. My relationship with those guys was basketball-related on the basketball court and in the locker room.

"Once we left practice, they did what they had to do. And I went my own separate way, I guess. I started off slow, but by the end of my freshman year, I started to have better numbers. After a big game on Friday night, you beat a rival, guys were going out and I was going home."

By his sophomore year, however, Hill no longer worried about his place within the South Lakes team. He had grown more than two inches, to six-feet, six-inches and his basketball game was blossoming.

"Dunking on people, handling the ball, playing a point forward – really able to dominate games," Hill said. "That's when it became easy.

"The perception is the best ball in the city [is in the District]. One of the things I liked about South Lakes was we wanted to be number one in the area. We played a little exhibition against Dunbar and we smacked them. We had something to prove. We didn't play a lot of city teams -- that's something I wish we had done more of. I know I carried a little chip on my shoulder and I think some of my teammates did as well."

Handling their Northern Virginia competition wasn't as challenging for the Seahawks. South Lakes waltzed through the 1987-88 regular season, losing just twice. Hill averaged twenty points in victories over Chantilly and Herndon to help the Seahawks win their holiday tournament. The Seahawks then repeated as Great Falls District champions, scoring a 71-69 victory over Washington-Lee in a rematch of the district final.

South Lakes was 21-2 and ranked seventh in the Washington area by The Washington Post before its season ended disappointingly in a 71-69 loss to Chantilly in the first round of the Northern Region tournament. The Chargers had entered game with an 11-11 record.

Hill averaged 21.2 points for the season and was emerging as a superstar. The recruiting letters from college coaches were coming daily.

The Northern Virginia Hawks won the sixteen-and-under AAU national title the next summer. Then, before the season started for South Lakes, Hill narrowed his potential college choices to North Carolina, Duke, North Carolina State, Michigan, Villanova, Pittsburgh, Georgetown, Virginia, Wake Forest and Notre Dame. The coaches at those schools would be seen early and often in Reston: At one December game, Maryland's Bob Wade, Duke's Mike Krzyzewski, Pittsburgh's Paul Evans and Wake Forest's Bob Staak all were in attendance.

Janet Hill, who worked at the Pentagon, wanted her son to go to Georgetown. Calvin Hill, then vice president of administration for baseball's Baltimore Orioles, preferred North Carolina, which is where all of the South Lakes players figured Grant Hill was going to college. Byrd laid down strict rules for the colleges on Hill's list; all contact was to come through Byrd and practices were closed to recruiters.

Just after Christmas, the Seahawks lost, 66-59, in a high-profile game to Archbishop Molloy of New York City and its star point guard, Kenny Anderson, in the first round of the Beach Ball Classic in Myrtle Beach, South Carolina. Hill had eighteen points and eleven rebounds, Anderson scored twenty-six points.

Later in the season, before a game against neighboring rival Herndon, Krzyzewski was walking into the gymnasium when he passed a few former South Lakes players, who jokingly wondered what the Duke coach was doing at the game.

"Man, Coach, he is not going to Duke," Williams-Baffoe said. "Duke is last on his list."

"Oh yeah?" Krzyzewski said, stopping to engage the group. "Why is he not going to go to Duke?"

Krzyzewski and the other college coaches knew what they were watching when Hill played. South Lakes was awesome that season, rising to Number One in The Post's rankings, winning all of their other regular season games. Hill was sensational. In the Northern Region championship game against Chantilly, he had twenty-four points and nine rebounds, making a key turnaround jumper while being fouled and then blocking a layup at the other end of the court in a 63-61 victory. It was the Seahawks' twenty-first consecutive victory.

Then, in the VHSL Group AAA tournament, teammate Rob Robinson had thirty points and eighteen rebounds in an 80-75 victory over Highland Springs, the first victory in the state tournament for South Lakes. Hill had nineteen points, twelve rebounds and eight blocked shots.

In the state semifinals against Hampton, Hill had twenty-five points and eleven rebounds, but the Seahawks' dream season came to a disappointing end. South Lakes made just thirteen of twenty-seven free throws in the 73-65 loss.

Having averaged nineteen points, ten rebounds and four blocks, Hill was named to The Post's All-Met team. That May, he narrowed his choices to Duke, Georgetown, Michigan, North Carolina, Stanford and Virginia.

Over the summer, Hill earned MVP honors at two Five-Star Basketball Camps. Then he set about trying to pick a college.

Subconsciously, though Georgetown was the toast of the Washington area at the time, Hill said he soured on the Hoyas because he felt it was too close to home and that Jackson had been held back during his college career. Virginia was dropped from consideration because it was announced that Coach Terry Holland would not return the next season.

"Virginia, they messed up, a lot of my friends went to U-Va. and I liked it a lot … [but] they never announced his replacement," Hill said. "Going into my senior year, I couldn't take them seriously because I didn't know who was going to be [coaching] there. From a recruiting standpoint, it was impossible for Terry Holland to recruit me. There is a chance that if he had stayed on, I might have gone there."

As he began visiting college campuses, Hill thought North Carolina would be his choice.

But when he went to Duke, something just clicked. During the trip, Hill called a friend who attended North Carolina and told her he was just up U.S. 15-501 in Durham.

Hill assured the friend that he was not going to Duke. "I'm just here on a visit," he said.

After being hosted by Duke standouts Christian Laettner and Brian Davis, though, Hill changed his mind.

"When I left, I felt this is where I wanted to be," Hill said. "It wasn't a great visit. It wasn't like they threw a huge party for me. It was just a great fit with the players, the school, Coach K -- everything. So when I got back from the trip, I wanted to cancel all my visits.

"But my dad was a really big Dean Smith fan, a big Carolina fan. Dean was coming in for an in-house visit two days later. Out of respect, I wanted to hear him out, see if I still felt that way."

The first college basketball game that Hill had intently studied was the 1982 NCAA tournament final, when freshman Michael Jordan's jump shot with fifteen seconds left gave North Carolina a 63-62 victory over Georgetown and Smith his first national title.

"We had Betamax, and I taped the game, and to this day I can still tell you every play that happened," Hill said. "But after Coach Smith came in, I still wanted to go to Duke."

Hill signed a National Letter-of-Intent to play for Duke before the season started, then went out and proved he was one of the nation's elite players.

In late January, Hill scored ten of his twenty-nine points in the fourth quarter of a 69-65 victory over Madison as South Lakes improved to 14-1, with thirty-five consecutive victories over Northern Region opponents. That streak ended when Hill sat out the regular season finale after injuring a foot in practice the previous day. There was no need to worry about Hill's foot; he came back and led the Seahawks to their fifth consecutive Great Falls District title, scoring twenty-nine points and grabbing twenty-three rebounds in a 65-62 victory over Madison in the district final.

That would be the only title that season for South Lakes. Hill had eighteen points and twelve rebounds in a 61-56 loss to Wakefield in the regional final, though both teams still advanced to the state tournament.

In the state tournament quarterfinals against Potomac, Hill had twenty-six points, sixteen rebounds and five assists in a 65-63 victory. Up next was a rematch with Hampton, but despite thirty-two points for Hill, South Lakes met the same result as the previous season. Hill scored 13 points in the final quarter as the Seahawks desperately tried to rally, but they never got closer than four points and lost, 81-66.

Hill finished his high school career with more than 2,000 points. He was named a McDonald's All-American and was The Post's All-Met Player of the Year, having averaged twenty-eight points, twelve rebounds, seven assists and four steals. In the Capital Classic, Hill had seventeen points, nine assists and five steals and shared MVP honors with Dunbar's Michael Smith after a 116-103 victory over the U.S. All-Stars.

No longer was Hill known as the son of a former NFL player. Now, Calvin Hill joked that he was known as the father of a rising basketball star.

Hill's high school career was just a starting point to a brilliant career. He played all five positions in his first game at Duke and quickly became a star on the college level. In the 1991 NCAA championship game, Hill helped limit Nevada-Las Vegas star Stacey Augmon to six points as the Blue Devils prevailed. The next season, in the NCAA tournament East Region final, Hill delivered one of the most famous assists of all time, hurling a seventy-five-foot inbounds pass to Laettner, who dribbled once, spun and sank a jump shot to beat Kentucky and propel Duke to another NCAA title. Nearly twenty years later, that remains one of college basketball's most memorable plays.

Hill finished his Duke career as the first played in Atlantic Coast Conference history with more than 1,900 points, 700 rebounds, 400 assists, 200 steals and 100 blocked shots.

"He was like the poster boy for college basketball because he was smart, he was good, he played a couple positions and he really handled the ball well," Maryland former coach Gary Williams said. "He was a clutch player. Duke was like a rock group at the time. He was never a great shooter, but a great player. He knew how to get to the paint, knew how to give it up. Today, he'd probably be a point guard if he was coming up in college now."

In the NBA, Hill was beset by ankle injuries, which required surgeries in three consecutive seasons and forced him to sit out one season while rehabbing. But he persevered. Drafted third overall in the 1994 NBA draft by the Detroit Pistons, Hill led all players in voting for the all-star game in his first two seasons in the league. He shared rookie of the year honors with Jason Kidd in 1994-95 and helped the United States to a gold medal in the Atlanta Olympics in 1996.

After six successful seasons in Detroit, in 2000 Hill signed a seven-year, ninety-two million dollar million contract to play for the Orlando Magic. It was in Orlando that Hill discovered the injury to his left ankle; he was not fully healthy until the 2004-05 season, when he returned to average 19.7 points. In 2007, Hill signed with the Phoenix Suns, where he played five seasons. He played for the Los Angeles Clippers in 2012-13 before retiring.

"Obviously, I put a lot of hard work and effort and time into it," Hill said. "I had good genetics -- a father who had pretty much experienced everything in sports, although a different sport. I actually think playing a different sport was good because I never felt I had to live up to him. If I played football, there would have been comparisons and I would have put pressure on myself, but I never did that.

"In order to have success and have done what I've done, you almost need to have a perfect storm. There are a lot of guys who I played with who had a lot of talent and I thought could go further, but didn't. To have a successful high school, college and long pro career, there is some luck involved, but there is a reason for it. It doesn't just happen. It's the experience in life, the lessons you learn -- it's a combination of many factors."

Hill is married to the former Tamia Washington, a singer he met on a blind date while playing for the Pistons. They have two children: Myla, and Lael.

4. Kevin Durant

Kevin Durant rarely hung out with friends. He never played friendly pickup games. Go to parties? See a movie? Forget it.

There was one place to find the skinny kid who loved playing basketball and everyone knew it: the Seat Pleasant Activity Center, on Addison Road in Seat Pleasant, Maryland.

"I was in the gym from eight in the morning until ten at night," Durant said. "Nobody wants to do that. But I just liked being there. I wasn't forced. It took a while for my skills to come around, but I kept at it and [local coach Taras Brown] kept pushing me."

It is almost difficult to fathom just how far Durant, born September 29, 1998, has come in such a short amount of time. It was only a few years ago that he was a smidge taller than six feet tall as he entered high school.

Since then, he sprouted like a weed to six-nine and became a star on every level.

As a senior at Montrose Christian School in Rockville, Maryland, Durant was The Washington Post's All-Met Player of the Year in 2005-06.

The next season, while a freshman at the University of Texas, Durant was college basketball's Player of the Year.

In 2007-08, while playing for the Seattle SuperSonics, Durant was the NBA Rookie of the Year.

In 2009-10, with the SuperSonics having relocated to Oklahoma City, Durant became the youngest player to lead the NBA in scoring, averaging 30.1 points per game. The next summer, after signing a five-year, eighty-six million dollar contract extension with the Oklahoma City Thunder, Durant led the United States to the gold medal in the world championships in Istanbul, Turkey.

"He has a chance to be one of the greatest players that ever played, because he has that work ethic and when it comes to a game situation he can get a shot up against anybody," said Stu Vetter, Durant's coach at Montrose Christian. "He has a great attitude and he does things the right way."

Indeed, in an era when professional athletes often are noted for their misbehavior or selfish attitudes, Durant is a rarity. Everybody, it seems, have only positive things to say about him.

Consider that when Durant agreed to the contract extension that should secure him financially for life, the player nicknamed KD released the news with a short post on his Twitter account. The next day, LeBron James, the self-proclaimed King James, held his much-maligned hour-long show, "The Decision," on ESPN.

Durant remains humble and quiet around outsiders. When hitting the court for practice, he follows the cliché: first one on the court and last one off. University of Maryland former coach Gary Williams remembers attending a workout of Montrose Christian players after Durant's rookie NBA season and seeing Durant take a charge against a high school player in a pickup game.

"How many guys in the NBA are going to do that?" Williams asked.

You better believe Durant got the call on that one.

Said Vetter a few years ago: "He went down to rookie camp in Orlando this past year. He didn't have to be there. And at six o'clock every morning, he's getting taped to practice with them at seven. He went there to work on drills! You don't do that when you're leading the league in scoring."

Kevin Durant might be one of the world's top five basketball players right now, but his work ethic remains as strong as ever.

For Durant, it all started one day in elementary school, when he approached his mother, Wanda Pratt, and told her he wanted to become a great basketball player. Pratt then approached Brown, who coached over at the activity center, and he designed a program for Durant to follow.

"Just to play with my friends, that is what drew me to the game," Durant said. "All my friends would play, and I wanted to be part of the group. Then it became a habit. I wanted to play every day. I wanted to get good. I wanted to be better than my friends. That is what drove me to be the player I am."

Durant's training regimen, though, was not always fun. He was not allowed to play pickup games with friends. Instead, there were drills, more drills and dozens and dozens of runs up a steep hill nearby. Occasionally, one of Durant's teammates from the Prince George's Jaguars would join in. More often than not, though, it was just Durant and Brown on the court.

"I always wanted to run around and play," Durant said. "It took me some time to really get used to it."

Occasionally, Durant grew so frustrated that he would start to cry, hoping that might end the part of the workout he considered torture.

"Most of the time, it wouldn't work," Durant said.

Brown was quick to reply, "Wipe off your face and run up that hill."

Equally unenjoyable was the exercise in which Brown would have Durant hold a medicine ball in a shooting position for long periods of time without moving. Sometimes Durant would be lying on his back on the gymnasium floor. Other times he was standing up, positioned to shoot.

"If I didn't do that, I had to go run the hills," Durant said.

Eventually, things started sinking in and Durant started to develop during middle school. Charlie Bell, a neighborhood buddy who played guard at National Christian Academy in Fort Washington, Maryland, told his coach, Trevor Brown, he should take a look at Durant. Brown then dispatched assistant coach Shawn Briggs to check out a Jaguars practice, where he saw a team that included Michael Beasley, Chris Braswell and Carl Scott.

Briggs returned with the same report Bell had delivered: "You need to come look at these kids. They're really good."

Brown invited the quartet to National Christian for an open gym. Braswell, a year younger, would be recruited the next year, though he ended up going to DeMatha Catholic High. Scott did not want to cut his long hair, Brown remembered, and instead went to his neighborhood public school, Largo High. Durant and Beasley, though, were obviously talented.

"I wanted these two kids here because they were pros," Brown said. "Both wore like size fifteen or sixteen shoes. Both had gigantic shoes. Probably the most skilled kids I've seen at that age in a long time."

Beasley enrolled at National Christian and stayed there one year. He bounced around five more high schools, had one spectacular year at Kansas State University and was the second overall pick in the 2008 NBA draft by the Miami Heat.

Durant's path to the NBA was not as bumpy, but it included a few twists and turns. The only private school other than National Christian to recruit Durant was Paul VI Catholic High in Fairfax, Virginia, but nothing materialized there. After starting the ninth grade at his local public school, Suitland High, a few weeks later Durant transferred to National Christian, where he joined the junior varsity team. It was quickly obvious, though, that Durant was ready for more of a challenge.

"He was holding his own against guys like Deron Washington, Patrick Ewing Jr.," Brown said.

After a handful of games, Durant moved up to the varsity squad. He averaged 2.7 points per game.

"But my sophomore year, I averaged seventeen," Durant said. "I grew like four or five inches. And I went from being the last man on the bench my freshman year to starting my sophomore year. I got better as time went on.

"My confidence grew a lot. Of course, I was taller and still had my guard skills. I was able to dribble and shoot and post up. I had the opportunity to stay on the court because I could do all those things. We had a lot of guys that were good."

Brown built National Christian into a perennially strong program, attracting attention from dozens of college recruiters. Washington went to Virginia Tech. Ewing headed to Indiana University before transferring to Georgetown University. Point guard Abdullah Jalloh started at St. Joseph's University before transferring to James Madison University.

But while college recruiters were already onto Durant, he would not complete his high school career at National Christian.

Oak Hill Academy, the tiny private school with perhaps the nation's best-known basketball team, was interested in Durant. Coach Steve Smith came to watch Durant play during the summer and invited him to come to southwestern Virginia and play for the Warriors.

"It was a dream of mine to go there," Durant said. "Oak Hill was one of the best basketball schools on any level. To play there with a lot of great players was something I wanted to do. And to get to live away from home, too. It was a great experience.

"It was tough for me to leave National. I wanted to stay and win at that school. But this was an opportunity I couldn't pass up. National exposure. Playing in front of lots of people on TV. There were more pros than cons. I had to take that opportunity. It prepared me for living away from home. Once I sat down and thought about it, it was a no-brainer."

After growing up around the Beltway in Prince George's County, spending a year in Mouth of Wilson, Virginia, was quite different.

"It was out in the woods, a secluded area. Very rural," Durant said. "The kids that go there are usually kids that get kicked out of the public schools in their cities. It was more of a secondary school. But everybody was nice and like a big family. They helped me a lot. We won the national championship there. To get a ring was an unbelievable feeling."

Still, Durant was one-and-done at Oak Hill. Wanda Pratt wanted the younger of her two boys closer to home. Tony Durant, two years older than Kevin, had spent his final three years of high school at St. John's Military School in Salina, Kansas. It was Tony who sparked Kevin's competitive fires growing up – whether it was playing one-on-one, playing video games or anything else. As Kevin prepared for his senior year of high school in the summer of 2005, having already decided to accept a scholarship offer from Texas Longhorns Coach Rick Barnes, he returned home, enrolling at Montrose Christian.

"My mom wanted me to come back home before I went to Texas, and I had to do what my mom wanted. I wanted to go to back to Oak Hill because I thought we had a good team and could win it all and graduate from there," Durant said. "I was a little upset at first when my mom told me I had to come back home. But that year was fun for me, playing back at home. Then to cap it off with us beating Oak Hill in the last game of the season on a buzzer shot was unbelievable."

That game, at Coolidge High in Northwest Washington, will go down as one of the most memorable ever played in the Washington area. Oak Hill's lineup included Beasley, guard Tywon Lawson (the 2009 Atlantic Coast Conference Player of the Year while playing for the University of North Carolina), guard Nolan Smith (a leader on Duke University's national championship team in 2010) and Virginia Tech standout forward Jeff Allen. Durant finished with thirty-one points and Lawson had twenty-six, but it was Maryland recruit Adrian Bowie who banked in a putback at the buzzer to give Montrose the 74-72 victory. Oak Hill finished the season with forty victories and one loss.

"What Kevin liked about us is the work ethic," Vetter said before leaving Montrose Christian following the 2012-13 season. "He was always there for our morning workouts. Sometimes we would work out at six-thirty in the morning and he was always there. A great player sometimes doesn't feel right if he doesn't work out. When Kevin drops by our school now, he wants to join in the workout."

Durant averaged 23.6 points, 10.2 rebounds and 2.6 blocks his senior season.

That was just a starting point. He averaged 25.8 points and 11.1 rebounds during the 2006-07 season at Texas, leading the Longhorns to the second round of the NCAA tournament. He was the first freshman to win several national Player of the Year awards.

"People used to tell me all the time, 'You don't know how good you are,' " Durant said. "I always talked down on myself. I never thought I could be good at all. Then I started realizing if I worked every day and continued to come out on the court and be a killer, as I call it, anything can happen. I started to see results my freshman year in college."

Again, it was one-and done for Durant, with little question that he was ready to turn professional.

The Portland Trail Blazers made Ohio State freshman center Greg Oden the first pick of the 2007 NBA draft. Durant went second to the SuperSonics. In his first five seasons in the NBA, Durant averaged 20.3, 25.3, 30.1, 27.7 and 28.0 points – the second and third seasons, with the franchise relocated to Oklahoma City, were the first time he wore the same jersey in consecutive seasons since his two seasons at National Christian, in 2002-03 and 2003-04. As of summer 2015, Durant is a five-time All-NBA First Team selection. He also was the 2014 NBA Most Valuable Player and led the Thunder to the 2012 NBA Finals. He helped the United States win the gold medal in the 2012 London Olympics.

Despite his success, Durant remains the same player and person he always has been. Eager to lace up his shoes, hit the floor and start playing.

"If I see a basketball on the court, I've got to shoot," Durant said. "If there is a game on TV, I have to watch. I'm competitive and I have to get better. I'm always going to enjoy the game."

3. Adrian Dantley

There were always questions and never a shortage of skeptics.

Sure, Adrian Dantley could dominate the competition. But what would happen to the burly kid – the one nobody can remember seeing dunk a basketball -- when he took the next step?

The critics dogged Dantley before he enrolled in high school and continued throughout his career.

Could the undersized, underwhelming, under-jumping forward continue to score?

But after tens of thousands of points and his induction into the Naismith Basketball Hall of Fame, Dantley has delivered an emphatic answer.

"When I was younger, I really didn't care," Dantley said. "But I started getting older and, you know, it was always like I had to prove myself every time I played a game. No matter what I accomplished. When I was in high school, I might have been an All-American my junior year and played in all-star games, but it was always, 'I don't know if he can do that at the next level.' But anytime I played against top players, I killed them."

At every level.

One longtime local basketball observer noted that if Adrian Dantley were coming out of college today, NBA teams might pass on him. After all, there aren't many six-foot, five-inch forwards who make a living playing in the paint in contemporary professional basketball.

Dantley, though, always found a way to succeed on the court.

Perhaps the one break that fell his way was just getting into DeMatha Catholic High. Growing up in Northeast Washington in the mid 1960s, as an eighth-grader Dantley played for the basketball team at Bertie Backus Junior High. Backus, which had students in seventh through ninth grades, had a game against the DeMatha freshman team. Legendary Stags Coach Morgan Wootten was in attendance to see another Backus player, Eugene Robinson.

"They wanted him -- nobody had heard of me," Dantley said. "I was in the background. I was a second-tier guy. I was pretty good, but I wasn't the guy. I wasn't the guy on that team."

That might have been the last time Dantley could make such a statement.

Regardless of where he rated on the Backus team, Dantley managed enough to stir interest from Wootten; Dantley already had plenty of interest in DeMatha. The Stags' current star, James Brown, lived just down Sargent Road from Dantley in Northeast Washington.

Finally, it was decided that Dantley could go to DeMatha, but on one condition: He had to take summer school classes in math and English. So did Robinson.

"He lasted two days and quit, but I persevered and stayed in summer school the whole six weeks and everything is history from then on," Dantley said. "My aunt [Muriel 'Rosie' Jenkins] was a schoolteacher and said I was going to go to school, come back, take a break and then study. At that time, all the kids were playing ball in the alley. The whole time, I couldn't go out in the alley until I got my work done.

"Fifteen guys were in the same boat I was in. Ain't too many of them [made it]. Out of fifteen, I think maybe three of them might have lasted."

As for Robinson, he went to Wilson High, a public school in Northwest Washington, and played for its team.

"He did all right," Dantley remembered. "Didn't go to college. Talented, but not as disciplined as Adrian Dantley."

Once at DeMatha, Dantley made an immediate impact. He became the first player in the history of the Hyattsville school to start on the varsity basketball team for four seasons.

And while Dantley, at thirteen, was somewhat of a role player his freshman year – Wootten told him to focus on grabbing rebounds – he was a star throughout his time at DeMatha.

Grab rebounds? That freshman year, Dantley matched the school record with thirty-three in a single game. (That record, obviously, was soon to be broken.)

Dantley wasn't daunted by playing older, more experienced opponents. He had been doing that for some time on the playgrounds outside Monroe Elementary and Banneker Junior High in the District.

"I used to get jumped because I beat [older] guys at one-on-one," Dantley said. "When I used to ride around there when I was in college, I would see some guys and stop and say, 'Remember, you used to beat me?' They'd say, 'I don't remember.' It seemed like they were the same height then as they were when we played!"

Of course, Dantley always was taller than most of those opponents. As a ninth-grader, he averaged eleven points and eleven rebounds. He made the game-winning layup in the closing seconds to beat Cardozo, 61-60, in the M Club doubleheader at Cole Field House and relished a victory over second-ranked Eastern the next night.

"Adrian was an enigma to me; I couldn't figure out how he could score," said former Georgetown University Coach John Thompson, who first saw Dantley that freshman year, when Thompson was coaching at rival St. Anthony's High. "Adrian is right up there with Rabbit [Elgin Baylor] and [Dave] Bing because of what he could do. He had the unusual ability to score on people who were almost two times his size on the inside."

But that first year at DeMatha was just the start of things for Dantley.

Having grown tired of being asked when he would use his muscular body on the football field, Dantley joined the Stags' football team as a sophomore and made the Metro Conference's all-league team as a defensive end.

Then basketball season started.

In the first four games, Dantley averaged 24.8 points and 17.5 rebounds. He then made the game-tying layup with four seconds left in regulation and made a free throw with two seconds remaining in a 68-67 victory over Bishop Eustace Preparatory School of Pennsauken, N.J. At season's end, the Stags had twenty-nine victories and two losses, and Dantley held the school single-game record with thirty-four rebounds in one game. He was the only sophomore named to The Washington Post's All-Met team.

"I'd score a lot on the inside and from seventeen [feet] and in," Dantley said. "It was always, 'He's not going to do that at the next level.' No matter what level I was at, it was, 'He's good, but I don't believe he's going to do that at the next level.' "

Said DeMatha teammate Pete Strickland, who went on to a lengthy coaching career: "He was earthbound, but so technically correct and fundamental that it was nauseous. I don't think I ever saw him dunk. You'd be hard-pressed to find anybody in D.C. who saw him dunk. But he was so thick and used his body so well."

Dantley, though, disputes the notion that he could not dunk.

"The first time I dunked a basketball was when I was in junior high, when I was six-two," he said. "The thing you hear about me, guys always used to say they never saw Adrian dunk. I used to always say, 'That's why I can walk right now.' I never had any knee injuries.

"I never worried about making the fancy play. I tell people all the time, I could have been one of the most flamboyant and flashiest players of all time, but I wouldn't have been productive. My thing was being efficient. That's what my game was all about. I talk to players today and there is no way in the world I would shoot forty percent from the floor. I wouldn't take those kind of shots. I wouldn't be a volume shooter."

One of the few things he did in volume – besides play basketball – was exhibit an unusual dedication to conditioning and strength training.

He had been introduced to the weight room at Bertie Backus. Back then, Dantley had the nickname "Baby Fats." When he enrolled at DeMatha, Dantley was six-feet, three-inches and weighed two hundred twenty-five pounds.

"I had the ass, big thighs. I wasn't obese -- just a little chunky," Dantley said. "But then, all basketball players were toothpicks back then, six-five, one-eighty-five or so."

Some teasingly called him "Baby Huey."

"A lot of them, they got a kick out of calling me that because I killed them all the time" on the court, Dantley said. "That was the only thing they could come back with and try to make me feel bad."

Throughout high school, though, Dantley showed an unwavering commitment to training. Basketball players rarely lifted weights, often concerned that it might hurt their shooting touch. But Dantley was a regular in the weight room.

"It used to be: 'You'll get too musclebound, you'll get too tied up,'" Wootten said. "I didn't know anything about [lifting weights], but I told him if he wanted to learn more, we could go up to Maryland and meet with the strength coach. We bumped into [Tom] McMillen up there. That wasn't the 'in' thing then. How many ninth-graders would have the moxie to dive into something like that? He knew then what he wanted to be."

And during the summer, he would run the steps at the University of Maryland's Byrd Stadium on a daily basis. In cooler weather, Dantley would run indoors, in Cole Field House.

"I did that for conditioning, but I also did that because everybody said you're going to jump high if you do that," Dantley said. "I did everything I could to get a vertical leap. But that didn't work for me."

Craig Esherick, who was then a student at Springbrook High before going on to play at Georgetown and succeed Thompson as its coach, remembers walking past Byrd on a day he thought was too hot to play basketball outdoors. But there was Dantley, bouncing up one series of steps after the next.

"That's the kind of work ethic he had," Esherick said. "Everybody in the area knew how hard he worked. He was a great inside player as a ninth-grader, but then he lost all that weight and chiseled himself into a power forward. He made himself into a great player."

Dantley's final two years at DeMatha were even more spectacular than his first two, as the Stags won fifth-nine games and lost two.

As a junior, he was an all-league tight end in football, then continued rolling on the basketball court. Among the highlights were a forty-three point outing in a victory over All Hollows of New York City in the O'Connell holiday tournament and a thirty-eight point, twenty-eight rebound effort in a 93-70 victory over Good Counsel that clinched a fifth consecutive Metro Conference title. Former Boston Celtics coach Red Auerbach compared him to Baylor.

Again, Dantley made The Post's All-Met team. After the season, as was his policy for rising seniors, Wootten finally showed Dantley the endless pile of recruiting letters sent by college coaches. Four schools wound up making the final cut: Maryland, Notre Dame, North Carolina and Minnesota.

The current trend is for players to make their college choices earlier and earlier in the recruiting process, often creating situations that prompt the player or college to change their minds. But Dantley took his time.

Dantley, along with his mother, Virginia Dantley, and her sister, Rosie, enjoyed the recruiting process. Dantley especially took a liking to Maryland Coach Lefty Driesell, who perhaps was the only coach never to doubt Dantley.

Driesell, always regarded as a most creative recruiter, did everything he could to land the DeMatha High superstar.

"Stay here in D.C.," Driesell made his pitch. "I need somebody that can guard [North Carolina State star] David Thompson and you can do it."

Driesell would go to the wharf in Southwest Washington to buy fresh seafood, then drive through Dantley's neighborhood and wonder what he was doing there. After pickup games in Cole Field House with Maryland's players and others, Dantley often would retire to a steam room, where Driesell would join him.

"One time we were in there so long, we must have lost ten pounds each," Dantley said. "At least."

"I recruited him very hard," Driesell said. "He was my number one prospect."

Dantley opted to skip his senior year of football and focused on basketball. He scored a sensational thirty-six points in a 71-68 victory over Carroll that required double overtime, and the Stags stretched their winning streak to forty-three games before an 85-71 loss to Dunbar High of Baltimore.

Then, in the first City Title Game since 1962 – the game had been cancelled after a riot following that year's City Title football game between Eastern High and St. John's College High – Dantley had twenty points and ten rebounds in an 89-77 victory over Western High. Not surprisingly, he was again named All-Met.

After the season, he scored twenty-five points and grabbed twelve rebounds and was named the U.S. All-Stars' most valuable player in an 87-74 victory over the Pennsylvania All-Stars in the Dapper Dan Roundball Classic in Pittsburgh. Dantley made seven of eight shots and eleven of twelve free throws.

His high school career complete, Dantley finally made his college choice in mid-June.

He had visited Indiana University, where Bobby Knight was in his second season coaching the Hoosiers.

"I don't care what you do," Dantley remembered Knight telling him. "But if you don't go to Indiana, don't go to f----- Minnesota!"

Knight, it seems, did not get along with the Golden Gophers' coach, Bill Musselman.

Dantley also visited Southern California and Nevada-Las Vegas. He especially got a kick out of the Running Rebels' new coach, Jerry Tarkanian.

"He was recruiting me, [but] he was recruiting six guys to play the same position," Dantley said. "I said, 'I'll never get the ball with these guys.'"

Having narrowed his choices, Dantley was on the fence with Maryland and nearly succumbed to Driesell's persistent recruiting and his charm.

"I'd be outside jumping rope and I'd turn around and Lefty would be there," Dantley said. "I told him, 'Coach, I like Maryland, but I want to go away. I don't want to stay home.'"

Driesell, naturally, took the hint. He showed up the next day with a suitcase and red-and-white Maryland jersey with Dantley's name on the back, ready for him to wear once he arrived in College Park. That nearly did the trick. Dantley had scratched Maryland from the list but quickly called Wootten to make sure he had yet to say anything to Driesell; the Terrapins were still in consideration.

Dantley also was tempted to go to North Carolina, where former DeMatha assistants Eddie Fogler and Terry Truax were assistants to Dean Smith. Dantley had attended Smith's camp for several summers. But he didn't like Smith's slowing down the game with his "four corners" offense.

North Carolina State tried to convince him that David Thompson could be moved to guard, opening a forward slot for Dantley. "Okay, right," Dantley said. "That's why you've got to have some common sense, too."

Finally, in mid-June, Dantley opted for Notre Dame.

Although Coach Digger Phelps had arranged for Dantley to meet with Austin Carr, a Washington native and former Notre Dame standout, Dantley said a visit to the South Bend, Indiana, campus swayed his mind.

"I wasn't even really that interested in Notre Dame at all," Dantley said. "I was only interested in Notre Dame because Austin Carr went there. Also, they were always on television, even though it was a football school. But then one year they were like six and twenty."

That was Phelps's first season, 1971-72. Phelps, though, was able to overcome that dismal season and persuade Dantley to take a look at joining the stream of Washington-area players who went to Notre Dame, a list that included Carr, one-time DeMatha standouts Sid Catlett and Bob Whitmore and former St. John's standout Collis Jones.

"That was the last school I visited," Dantley said. "I came down the street, saw the Golden Dome. [Phelps] didn't really recruit me. I just said, 'I'm going to go to Notre Dame.'"

Just as with DeMatha, Dantley found instant success at Notre Dame. As a freshman, he scored nine points as the Fighting Irish ended UCLA's eighty-eight-game winning streak with a 71-70 victory.

Dantley went on to be a two-time All-American. The U.S. Basketball Writers Association presented him with the 1976 Oscar Robertson Trophy winner as the national Player of the Year. Before skipping his senior season to enter the NBA draft, Dantley had scored 2,223 points, second-most of any Notre Dame player.

Dantley was the sixth overall pick in the 1976 NBA draft, selected by the Buffalo Braves. Before going on to win NBA Rookie of the Year honors, though, he led the U.S. Olympic team to the gold medal that summer in Montreal. (Boxer Sugar Ray Leonard, from Palmer Park, Maryland, also won gold at the Summer Games.)

In workouts for the Olympic team, Dantley hardly was imposing. He was terrific in the spotlight, but he was not as special during practice.

"I've had a lot of coaches tell me if you come to practice and if you see Adrian Dantley practice sometimes, you wouldn't think he could play basketball," Dantley said.

Such was the case that summer at North Carolina as the Olympic team prepared. But while some coaches were concerned, Thompson – serving as an assistant to Smith – convinced them otherwise.

"You hear about some players who are great in practice and when the popcorn starts popping, they don't want to play," Dantley said. "I was the opposite. I didn't get embarrassed – I played hard – but you just didn't see anything special [from me] in practice. ... I always paced myself. A lot of coaches didn't like that."

Nothing changed once Dantley joined the NBA, as he contined to be a scoring machine. He played fifteen seasons in the league, seven with the Utah Jazz. He was named an NBA all-star six times and led the league in scoring in 1980-81 and 1983-84. In those two seasons and the two in between, Dantley averaged more than thirty points per game.

It was during his pro career that Dantley famously would look around town for preseason competition each fall, usually playing full-court games of one-on-one or two-on-two against top high school or college players.

"I used to break people down," Dantley said. "We'd lift weights and after lifting weights, I knew they'd be dead and wouldn't have nothing left."

Said Maryland former coach Gary Williams: "He had the reputation that his workout routine in the offseason was ridiculous. Guys would come into town and work out with him for a day and leave. He was Charles Barkley before all the publicity. He could score against anybody, even though he was six-five at most."

Dantley retired with a career scoring average of 24.3 points per game, shooting fifty-four percent from the field and 81.8 percent from the foul line.

Dantley and his wife, Dinitri, have been married more than thirty years. They have three children: Cameron, who played football at Syracuse University; Kalani; and Kayla. Dantley was an assistant coach for the Denver Nuggets for eight seasons.

And that work ethic? It continues to be strong. Dantley works as a Montgomery County crossing guard and has started to referee high school basketball games.

2. Dave Bing

Has any basketball player from the Washington area made a bigger impact that Dave Bing?

Forget about all the on-court accolades. All-Met at Spingarn High in Northeast Washington. All-everything at Syracuse University. NBA rookie of the year in 1967. Seven-time NBA all-star. His number 21 jersey retired by the Detroit Pistons. A spot on the NBA's list of Fifty Greatest Players

That stuff is all nice.

But then think about what Dave Bing has accomplished *after* retiring from basketball.

Learning from the ground up how to be a businessman. Forming a company that within five years had revenue of forty million dollars. Being named National Minority Small Business Person of the Year by the president of the United States.

That's nice, too.

Then, in his late sixties, Bing tackled his biggest challenge. Sensing there was no one capable who was interested in doing the job, he became the mayor of Detroit, trying to save the nation's eleventh-largest city from a variety of ills.

"I try to lead by example," Bing said. "Go back to when I was eleven or twelve years old, playing on a baseball team. I was the first guy there, the last guy to leave. It was the same thing in college and the pros, business and now politics. I'm not afraid of hard work. I want to put in the time and effort. I'm not willing to ask people to do something I'm not doing."

Want to pinpoint where that resourcefulness and work ethic comes from?

147

Go back to far Northeast Washington in the late 1940s, near what is now H.D. Woodson High School. Dave was the second of four children; his father was a bricklayer and his mother was a housewife.

Without much to do, the five-year-old boy tried to entertain himself. He took a few two-inch-by-two inch pieces of lumber and nailed them together, imitating what his father might do with a hammer, some wood and a few nails.

"When you're poor, you just figure out what kind of games you can play," he said. "In the neighborhood I grew up in, at that age you weren't allowed to go to the playground. You had to figure out what you could do in your neighborhood to have fun. A lot of kids, we had imaginations. I imagined I was a cowboy. I put two sticks together and acted as if it were my horse. I was running around and tripped.

"You're not worried about safety or anything like that. The nail wasn't banged in all the way. It hit me in my left eye."

The pain was sharp, but with the family lacking money or insurance, there was not much that could be done. Ever since, he has had blurred vision.

"I don't think my parents even understood the severity of the accident," Bing said. "Even if they did, there was not a lot they could do. Without insurance, they didn't even take me to the hospital."

Not being able to see from one end of the basketball court to the other was never a deterrent. Although his siblings never became interested in sports, Dave could always be found on a court or in the field. Hasker Bing had played baseball, and Dave took after his father.

He would play three seasons on the Spingarn baseball team, moving from shortstop to center field to first base and batting nearly .400. But basketball was the sport of choice for teenagers in the District, and Bing was no different.

"The girls came to watch basketball -- they didn't come to watch baseball," Bing said. "I had a reason for moving toward basketball. And I didn't know any baseball players that got scholarships to college. At least with basketball, you could get a scholarship. Between the opportunity to get a scholarship to go to college and the girls following basketball, those were my reasons for sticking with basketball.

"It was the city game. Baseball and football were not the chosen sports. It was basketball for as long as I can remember, and I think it's still true today."

Usually, Bing would head over to the playground at Kelly Miller Junior High, where the lighted courts always drew a crowd. Sometimes he would go to Turkey Thicket in Northeast. Wherever he went, there was something about him that made others want to help. Older players, such as Sleepy Harrison, Dee Williams and Wil Jones, often provided on-court tutoring.

"As a youngster aspiring to play basketball, I was very fortunate that the older guys in the neighborhood took me under their wing,' Bing said. "They saw something in me. Plus, as a young guy, you had to pass them the ball. They needed someone they could control, who passed the ball and didn't worry about shooting all the time.

"That helped me early on to gain some skills and development that I would not have gained had I just played with my peer group."

Bing was not the first basketball star to go to Spingarn: That would be Elgin Baylor. But Baylor spent one season in a Green Wave uniform; Bing spent his high school career there, teaming with Ollie Johnson to lead Spingarn to consecutive Interhigh championships.

In 1960, before 10,500 – then the biggest crowd to see a Washington-area high school basketball game – the Green Wave lost the City Title Game to the legendary Archbishop Carroll Lions, 69-54, as John Thompson had twenty-three points and fifteen rebounds. Bing, a sophomore, had ten points.

The next year, Spingarn capped its season by ending top-ranked DeMatha's twenty-two game winning streak, 63-50, before 10,600 at Cole Field House. Bing scored seventeen of his twenty-two points in the second half to lead the Green Wave to its first city championship.

"That put Spingarn on the map," Bing said.

He averaged 16.2 points per game for Coach William Roundtree that season and made third-team All-Met. As a senior the next year, Bing averaged 16.9 points and was a first-team All-Met.

In early April of his senior year, he earned most valuable player honors in the All-Star High School Invitational in Allentown, Pennsylvania, on a team of players from the Washington area. It should not have been much of a surprise that the team was victorious, since there were four future NBA players on the roster: Bing, Jerry Chambers of Eastern, and John Austin and Johnny Jones of DeMatha.

"Long story short, we won the tournament, that's where I got recruited by Syracuse," Bing said. "I visited Syracuse as the last school I visited and was recruited by [football players] Ernie Davis and John Mackey. I was so impressed with those two guys. Syracuse had a horrible basketball team. They had lost twenty-seven consecutive games over a two-year period.

"I went there and a lot of people questioned my sanity. An All-American high school basketball player -- why would you go to a school so bad?"

But where others a struggling team, Bing saw opportunity, as he did at so many other stages of his life. He would have to play on the freshman team, but thereafter playing time was not going to be an issue.

"I had never left Washington," Bing said. "I knew I was good in the D.C. area, but when you are going away to college you don't know what to expect. If I had to do it all over again, I'd make the same decision."

And as he has done on other occasions, Bing and his teammates turned the Orangemen into winners. In the Hurricane Classic in Miami, on consecutive nights Bing led Syracuse to victories over Bill Bradley and Princeton and Rick Barry and host Miami. The quick, flashy guard scored 29 points in the championship victory. Bing averaged 22.2 points and 8.2 rebounds in his first season on the varsity; he also became good friends with fellow sophomore guard Jim Boeheim.

"We roomed together for two years. He was very thoughtful, very clean, very organized – the opposite of me," said Boeheim, who has been the Syracuse head coach since 1976 and was inducted into the Naismith Memorial Basketball Hall of Fame in 2005. "He used to look down on my side of the room with disdain.

"Obviously, there were a lot of black athletes at Syracuse at the time in football and basketball. Syracuse integrated quicker than most schools in the North. There were thirty, forty black athletes, at least, here then. He was the leader in the group.

"He just is a leader. Everybody tries to define that, they write books about it, I think. But some people just are leaders. People listen to and follow them. He was that leader from Day One. I don't think he consciously thinks, 'I'm the leader.' But he's the guy that you pay attention to and follow. He always has been.

"We were on the freshman team, but all the varsity players looked up to him, partly because of his talent but also the way he carried himself. He was the undisputed leader. He was captain of the team as a sophomore. I've been around a lot of great people, but he was one of a kind."

Bing led Syracuse in scoring in each of his three seasons, averaging 23.2 points as a junior and 28.4 points as a senior. An explosive point guard, he was ahead of his generation, knowing exactly how to weave to the basket and then use his athleticism to score.

"Dave had that God-given talent," said George Leftwich, who was two years older than Bing as they grew up on the city's basketball courts and went on to star at Carroll. "Most players have to dip to get up. But he was able to just *boing* and he's up there!"

Bing's success continued into the NBA. A second-round draft pick of the Detroit Pistons in 1966, he averaged twenty points and was rookie of the year. He retired after the 1977-78 season with career averages of 20.3 points and six assists – even with the inability to see clearly out of one eye.

"I had to really concentrate," Bing said. "I had a detached retina in my other eye in my fifth year. [But] I was still a twenty-plus guy a night. When I got the detached retina, only twenty-seven years old at the time, I knew if I could see again I wanted to play.

"The team doctor at the University of Michigan advised me not to play, because if I got hurt again I could go blind. But I came back. My game changed. After that injury, I had to pull back from being a perimeter player to being a true point guard and penetrating to the basket and getting the ball to other players. It was a different approach."

Maybe a different approach, but there was the same result. Bing was named an all-star eight times in his twelve seasons and was elected to the Naismith Memorial Basketball Hall of Fame in 1990.

By that time, his business career was in full swing.

Go find a modern-day player and tell him of Bing's offseason training – it had nothing to do with getting in the gym.

During his first seven years in the NBA, playing for the Pistons, Bing spent the summer working for the National Bank of Detroit. Then he worked three summers for Chrysler in a training program for car dealers. Finally, after retiring, he started Bing Steel, which found its niche as an automotive supply company, eventually growing from a company of four people into one that had 1,300 employees and revenue of three hundred million dollars.

"I envisioned myself one day owning my own business," Bing said. "I always read. Even as a star in the NBA, I was taught early on to be humble and never think you're better than somebody else because you have a gift. I always worked in the offseason. I knew I wasn't going to play basketball forever. I didn't know if I would have an opportunity to be a coach or general manager.

"There is much more satisfaction in starting a company, running a company, growing a company than there would have been being a coach or GM. I never looked at the sport as an end-all.

"I wanted to be the boss. I wanted to be the guy that made the final decision, that took the necessary risks. It all worked out for me. It wasn't easy, but it all worked out. ... I felt good about what I was doing. I was making a difference in the lives of a lot of people here in the city Detroit."

Interestingly, until his business career flourished, despite being from Washington, Bing had never been interested in politics. But with Bing Steel turning into the Bing Group and becoming a major economic venture, Bing got to know Detroit's leaders. Eventually, he became frustrated with the city's leadership and sought to become mayor after Kwame Kilpatrick resigned after becoming embroiled in a scandal.

Bing won a special election in 2009 and was re-elected to a full term later that year, serving as mayor through 2013.

"I think I was always anti-politics, but I knew the role politics played," Bing said. "I never thought about getting into politics ... [but] I didn't feel good about any leadership from a political standpoint."

Just as he always did on the basketball court and in other ventures, Dave Bing continued to lead by example.

1. Elgin Baylor

The best player ever from the Washington area was not as big a star as one might think during his high school playing days.

Not that Elgin Baylor was a late bloomer or somehow flew under the radar. It's just that in the early 1950s – back before the landmark Supreme Court case *Brown versus Board of Education* – Washington was a segregated city. When it came to high school basketball, the spotlight for the city's newspapers and other media outlets often did not shine on black-only schools or on black players.

So the player who changed the way the game was played, leaping – literally – toward the basket and showing that the game could be played above the rim, often took a back seat.

"Let's face it:. When you're put in a shell, you stay in that shell until it opens up. Baylor, in Washington, he got write-ups, but not that much," said Walter "Rock" Green, Baylor's teammate at Phelps High. "On a southern tour we would play Huntington [High of Newport News], [Armstrong High of] Richmond, Petersburg, Hampton, and he was a bigger star down there. He would have been a bigger star had he been white, no question.

"Baylor could do it all. People look and say about Dr. J [Julius Erving], but Elgin did that before Dr. J. He did that in high school, going from one side of the basket to the other and shooting. But he didn't do it with the style of Dr. J."

The Web site for the Naismith Memorial Basketball Hall of Fame concurs, noting that Baylor "was an innovative offensive force never before seen. . . . Baylor was the first athlete to play above the rim, paving the way for future leapers like Connie Hawkins, Julius Erving, and Michael Jordan."

There was not -- and still is not – any argument where Baylor ranked among his peers.

When creating a list of the Washington area's best players, Hall of Fame coach John Thompson said, "Number one is Elgin Baylor, then you skip down to number five and see who is next."

Born September 16, 1934, in Washington, Elgin was the youngest of three sons born to John and Uzziel Baylor. John was a steam engineer and Uzziel was a clerk at the U.S. Department of the Interior Department, according to a 1958 profile of Baylor in The Washington Post. Older brothers Kermit and Sal also were good basketball players.

Better known by the nickname, Rabbit, given to him by an uncle, Elgin played as a high school sophomore and junior at Phelps High, a vocational school in Northeast. He averaged 18.5 points as a sophomore in 1950-51 and 27.6 as a junior in 1951-52, – no small feat considering the low-scoring style of play at the time. He also set the school's single-game scoring record with forty-four points in a game against against Cardozo.

Just when most players would be ramping up for their senior year of high school, Baylor spent the next twelve months working in a furniture store and playing in local recreation leagues.

Think Kevin Durant, Michael Beasley, Chris Wright, Austin Freeman, Victor Oladipo or any of the other local stars fifty years later could be found selling sofas over at La-Z-Boy before their senior year?

When Baylor returned to school in the fall of 1953, he did so at Spingarn High, where the Green Wave was coached by Dave Brown, who had been Baylor's coach at Phelps. In just its second year of existence, Spingarn quickly had quite a record book in boys' basketball.

The Green Wave won the Interhigh Division II championship – Division I was for the District's white high schools, Division II for the black schools -- that year and Baylor quickly became a legend. On one February night, he scored sixty-three points against his former school, Phelps, tallying thirty-one in the first half and thirty-two after halftime despite playing with four fouls.

"Don't worry -- I'm not going to foul out," Baylor would tell any concerned teammates.

"And he never fouled out," Green said.

For the season, Baylor averaged 36.1 points per game and was named first-team All-Metropolitan by The Washington Post, spawning a generation of youngsters who tried to shoot on the run with one leg in the air.

"You know what it reminded you of?" Thompson said. "When a young kid can't reach the basket so you lift up one leg to push. Everybody would always try to copy that."

White players and black players would meet on the playgrounds, always playing a salt versus pepper game, but they almost never played in organized games.

The one time they did came in March 1954, according to a Washington City Paper story, after Baylor's Spingarn career had concluded, when the Washington Afro-American newspaper organized a game between Baylor's club team, the Stonewall Athletic Club, and a group of white high school players, led by high-scoring Jim Wexler of Western High.

"Here I am guarding Elgin Baylor one on one," Wexler told the City Paper of the game in which Baylor scored forty-four points and Wexler had thirty-four. "And he showed me basketball at a totally different level -- another world, heads and shoulders above anything I'd ever seen. He could do everything. He was a scorer. He could jump out of the gym. He reverse-dunked on me! You have to remember: Nobody did that before Elgin Baylor. That's not how basketball was played before him."

While his ability never was questioned, Baylor's college options were limited.

"They always said I had bad grades and that was bull," Baylor told the Seattle Post-Intelligencer in 2008. "I never got a grade below a C. None of the white scouts came to our games."

Baylor could have gone to Virginia Union University in Richmond, but he opted to take an athletic scholarship to the College of Idaho, where it was expected he would play basketball and football – even though he had never played high school football.

More than half a century later, football coaches still see tall, athletic teenagers on the basketball court and envision them excelling on the football field. Just look at former Eleanor Roosevelt High standouts Jared Gaither and Derrick Harvey, who starred in college and went on to play in the National Football League despite not playing that sport until later on in high school.

Regardless of why his options were limited, in the fall of 1954 Baylor found himself on a train to Caldwell, Idaho, some thirty miles west of Boise. A friend from Washington, Warren Williams, already played basketball there and helped line things up for Baylor.

Any thoughts of seeing the six-foot, six-inch Baylor on the football field, however, quickly disappeared, for he never suited up. No matter. On the basketball court, Baylor was amazing. He averaged 31.3 points his freshman year and was named an NAIA All-American. He still holds five school records established that season, including the single-game scoring mark of fifty-three points set against the Whitman Missionaries.

Even though he played in the southwestern corner of Idaho against less-than-top competition, Baylor was such a standout that he attracted the attention of Seattle car dealer Ralph Malone. A prominent booster at Seattle University, he convinced Baylor to transfer schools. The NCAA still had rules that mandated transfers had to sit out a season of competition, but clearly the association's amateurism and recruiting regulations were a bit different then; while sitting out, Baylor played for an AAU team sponsored by one of Malone's car dealerships.

Finally eligible at Seattle, Baylor again made an immediate impact. He played two seasons for the Chieftains. In 1956-57, as a redshirt sophomore, he led the nation in rebounding (20.3 per game) and was third in scoring (29.7 points per game). The following year, as a redshirt junior, he was second nationally in scoring to Oscar Robertson (32.5 points per game), although his rebounding dropped to a measly 19.3 per game! Against Pacific Lutheran, Baylor tallied fifty-one points and thirty-seven rebounds. He made a thirty-foot shot to beat San Francisco in the NCAA tournament West Regional and took Seattle all the way to the NCAA tournament championship game in 1958, where the Chieftains lost to the Kentucky Wildcats, 84-72.

Baylor could have returned to Seattle for one more season, but because he was in his fourth year of college, he exercised his right to turn professional.

The Minneapolis Lakers selected Baylor first overall and coaxed him to sign a contract with a twenty-five thousand dollar signing bonus.

Baylor was the NBA Rookie of the Year in 1958-59, averaging 24.9 points, fifteen rebounds and 4.1 assists per game as he led the previously last-place Lakers to the NBA Finals. In his second season, Baylor scored an NBA single-game record sixty-four points against the Boston Celtics. The following season, in November 1960, he topped that mark, scoring seventy-one points in a victory over the New York Knicks.

Perhaps Baylor's most impressive season came in 1961-62, when he averaged 38.3 points in forty-eight games while playing only on weekends after being called to active duty as a U.S. Army reservist. Baylor would fly -- coach, no less -- from his base at Fort Lewis south of Seattle, Washington, on weekend passes to play with the Lakers, then return to the base. The sixty-one point outing he had against the Boston Celtics still stands as the most points ever scored in a game in the NBA Finals.

Not that everything was a cakewalk for Baylor.

There was the time his rookie season, when the Lakers traveled to Charleston, West Virginia, for a preseason game only to have Baylor and the team's two other black players told they could not stay in the same hotel or eat at the same restaurants as their white teammates.

Then there was night in 1960, when the team's DC-3 charter plane miraculously crash-landed in a snow-covered cornfield in Carroll, Iowa, -- miraculously without any injuries.

Baylor's terrific career continued as the Lakers moved to Los Angeles in 1961, though he began having knee problems during the 1963-64 season. In thirteen seasons, he was selected to play in eleven all-star games and ten times made the All-NBA team – even though the Lakers never won an NBA championship during his career, losing in the Finals eight times.

Nine games into the 1971-72 season, Baylor decided that the pain in his knees was too great to overcome and he retired. The Lakers won their next thirty-three games en route to their first league championship in eighteen years.

In 846 career games, Baylor scored 23,149 points, grabbed 11,463 rebounds and had 3,650 assists.

He was elected to the Naismith Memorial Basketball Hall of Fame in 1977 and was named to the NBA's 35th and 50th anniversary teams.

Baylor spent three seasons coaching the New Orleans Jazz, compiling a record of 86 victories and 135 losses before leaving the bench after the 1978-79 season.

He later moved into the front office, hired as the general manager of the woeful Los Angeles Clippers in 1986, a position he held until 2008.

Although his playing career was nearly unmatched, for many newer fans the lasting image of Baylor is his near-annual appearance at the NBA Draft during his twenty-two years as the Clippers' general manager.

He should be remembered in a different light.

Acknowledgements

Trying to find and interview the Capital Kings was an interesting challenge. Some were easy to locate, others more difficult.

Nearly all were accommodating and generous with their time.

The idea for this book came from Bob Geoghan, who made his mark in the high school basketball world by creating and successfully running the Capital Classic and McDonald's All-American Game. Over the years, work occasionally took me in Bob's direction and to Dan O'Neil, one of his former trusted employees, who has become a good friend.

Then came the next question: Could it be pulled off?

Fortunately, Bob has a remarkable memory. Between his contacts and mine, we were able to form quite an unofficial list of advisers to help pick the team.

The research was fascinating. Having graduated from high school in 1990 (Springbrook High in Silver Spring, Maryland – which does not have a player on the list!), I was not well acquainted with many of the players on the list. Although I wrote for The Washington Post for nearly seventeen years – five covering University of Maryland football and men's basketball, the rest covering local high school sports – my first-hand knowledge was limited.

After all, when it came time to finish the list, only two players were still playing. Kevin Durant of the Oklahoma City Thunder made time after returning from Turkey where he led the United States to the FIBA World Championship. Reaching Louis Bullock was more difficult. I found on Facebook the public relations representative for his professional team in Spain and sent her a message – in Spanish. Fortunately, Virginia Simon Ballesteros was like most of the other people I encountered extremely helpful and pledged to give my message and phone number to Louis. Eventually, we spoke and he could not have been more gracious. Although Louis is fluent in Spanish and Italian from playing overseas his entire pro career, we spoke in English.

To learn about the other players, I leaned on anyone I could: former players, coaches, teammates and friends.

Facebook proved invaluable, for I tracked down dozens of people who have scattered throughout the United States.

Most of the players were interviewed in person. Grant Hill, the ageless forward at the time playing for the Phoenix Suns, scheduled an interview for a Sunday morning when he was back in town. As we said goodbye in a hotel lobby, Grant explained why he was in Washington that weekend – to play basketball with President Obama and attend a barbecue at the White House. I sent a note to Post White House correspondent Mike Shear, figuring he knew of this event but wanting to be sure. Naturally, the White House PR staff had not let on that Obama was hosting Hill and a few dozen stars for a pickup game. For a few hours, I had a byline on the lead story about the president's daily activities. Pretty cool.

I also got a story for The Post when I located Sherman Douglas. Nearly ten years after retiring from the NBA, he and fellow graybeard Mark Tillmon – regarded as one of the finest ever to don a Gonzaga Eagles uniform – were playing in what used to be the Kenner League at Georgetown with the teenagers and twenty-somethings.

I drove to Durham, North Carolina, to interview Johnny Dawkins, who now coaches at Stanford University in Palo Alto, California, but still maintains a home just off Tobacco Road. While waiting to meet Dawkins in a shopping mall parking lot, I phoned Wil Jones, the former 1950s Dunbar High star who now spends half the year living in Virginia Beach. Wil has a bad back and had been difficult to nail down for an interview. I told him that after interviewing Johnny, I was driving to Virginia Beach to talk with him. At that moment, Johnny pulled up. Of course, Wil asked to speak with Johnny, who must have thought I was crazy as I handed him the phone and said someone wanted to speak with him.

My three hours with Wil will go down as one of the most memorable interviews of my career; he was so passionate when speaking that he would make the painful effort to get up, point his finger and occasionally prod me just to be certain I understood how strongly he felt. I feel fortunate to have spent that time with Wil; he passed away in 2015.

By the way, I was floored by Wil's connection to seemingly everyone on the list – lending a car to Lew Luce, giving Adrian Dantley his first basketball, and so on.

I still shake my head in amazement at what Elgin Baylor and Dave Bing accomplished, though I was disappointed Elgin declined interview requests while working on his own book. I am certain that will be a must-read.

Other old-timers who could tell stories about former players included Lefty Driesell, Joe Gallagher (who passed away in 2014), Jim Phelan and Morgan Wootten. Such coaches as Todd Bozeman, Paul DeStefano, Craig Esherick, Red Jenkins, Keith Stevens, Pete Strickland and Stu Vetter had plenty of stories to tell from their decades of local involvement in the game. Then there is Tom Ponton, DeMatha High's director of development, a walking encyclopedia on all things DeMatha, with a rolodex to match.

John Thompson and Gary Williams, the coaches who turned Georgetown and Maryland into national champions, also were generous with their time and candid with their stories. I was especially appreciative of them.

Stacy Robinson's honesty and forthrightness were an eye-opener. I might be wrong, but I felt like he had gotten a load off his shoulders by telling his story on a crowded Sunday afternoon at Union Station.

Nearly all of the public relations workers I dealt with went beyond the call of duty to help double-check facts. As you can imagine, trying to remember events that happened dozens of years ago is not easy for the players.

Colleagues and friends such as Steve Argeris, Alan Goldenbach, Sheldon Shealer and Mark Thomas often read rough drafts and gave invaluable feedback, such as when Mark dug into the Wayback Machine to when he was a student in the late 1980s at Laurel High and remembered watching Ernie Cage referee games.

Tim Warren, a former Post colleague, was a terrific help editing the book. A basketball junkie with a keen sense of the region's hoops history, he was a natural choice to edit and guide the book.

I've been more than lucky throughout my career to have worked for editors who were more than willing to point a former American Studies major in the right direction. That list includes Scott Briscoe, Neil Greenberger, Steve Berkowitz, Matt Rennie, Drew van Esselstyn, Jon DeNunzio, Dan Uthman, Micah Pollack and Camille Powell. I never could thank longtime Post sports boss George Solomon enough for giving me a chance to prove myself in the first place.

There also were dozens of (mostly) former colleagues kind enough to teach a youngster some tricks, including: Mark Asher, Dave Sell, Richard Justice, Ken Denlinger, Len Shapiro, Bill Gildea and Michael Wilbon.

Finally, I am most thankful to my wife, Jodi, who spent many nights as a single mother as I headed off to write while she took on the task of persuading Sasha and Chelsey to go to sleep.

I am certain that I have forgotten some folks without whose advice, suggestions, connections or other guidance things would have been much more difficult. To them, I apologize, but I know that I am appreciative.

ROBERT J. GEOGHAN
Creator and publisher of Capital Kings

Bob Geoghan grew up living in NE Washington, DC beginning in the 40's. Over the past 65 years he has witnessed some of the best high school basketball teams and players during that time. Wanting to share his thoughts on who might be the 25 greatest high school hoopsters who ever played in the DC/MD/VA area he has teamed up with former Washington Post writer Josh Barr to produce "CAPITAL KINGS"

Geoghan founded the Capital Classic in March 1974 at the newly opened Capital Centre in Prince George's County. It was a high school all star basketball game featuring the best prep seniors from the Washington D.C. area against the top high school stars from all over the United States.

That game, which featured Moses Malone, drew 11,000 fans which allowed Geoghan to turn his passion for sports, creating events, and developing mutually beneficial relationships into a 40-year career in event management and marketing.

The Capital Classic will celebrate its 40th anniversary event in 2013.

The Capital Classic led the way to his creating the McDonald's All American Basketball Team in 1977 and launching the inaugural McDonald's All American Game in 1978.

The McDonald's All American Games will celebrate its 36th anniversary event in Chicago on April 3, 2013

He also founded the Washington Metropolitan Basketball Hall of Fame in 1983.

Geoghan lives in Laytonsville, Maryland with his wife Shirley. He has 3 children Tracy, Sean and Stephanie. He has 5 grandchildren Emily(13), Nolan(10), Alex(6), Brianna(5) and Jack(3)

He wishes to acknowledge the support from friends Mike Richard, Jerry O'Leary and Pennington Greene. He was inspired to publish this book by his friend Ronny Watts who played at Wilson High School (1961) where he averaged 20 points and 21 rebounds his senior year, played college ball at Wake Forest (1965) where averaged a double/double and led the ACC in total rebounds, and professionally with the Boston Celtics (1965-1967) before suffering a career ending knee injury.

Geoghan can be contacted at robertjgeoghan@aol.com

Made in the USA
Monee, IL
24 March 2021

63666465R00104